International Library of Psychol
Philosophy and Scientific Meth

Tractatus Logico-Philosophicus

Tractatus
Logico-Philosophicus

By
LUDWIG   WITTGENSTEIN

With an Introduction by
BERTRAND RUSSELL, F.R.S.

ROUTLEDGE & KEGAN PAUL LTD
LONDON AND NEW YORK

First published in this Series 1922
by Routledge & Kegan Paul Ltd.
11 *New Fetter Lane, London EC4P 4EE*

Published in the USA By
Routledge and Kegan Paul Inc.
in association with Methuen Inc.
29 *West 35th Street, New York NY*10001
Reprinted (with corrections) 1933
Reprinted 1947, 1949, 1951
Reprinted (with an Index) 1955
Reprinted 1958, 1960, 1962, 1971
Reprinted and First Published as a Paperback in 1981
Reprinted in 1983, 1985 *and* 1986
Printed in Great Britain by
Redwood Burn Limited, Trowbridge, Wiltshire

ISBN 0 7100 3004 5
ISBN 0 7100 0962 3 (P)

NOTE

In rendering Mr Wittgenstein's Tractatus Logico-Philosophicus *available for English readers, the somewhat unusual course has been adopted of printing the original side by side with the translation. Such a method of presentation seemed desirable both on account of the obvious difficulties raised by the vocabulary and in view of the peculiar literary character of the whole. As a result, a certain latitude has been possible in passages to which objection might otherwise be taken as over-literal.*

The proofs of the translation and the version of the original which appeared in the final number of Ostwald's Annalen der Naturphilosophie (1921) *have been very carefully revised by the author himself; and the Editor further desires to express his indebtedness to Mr F. P. Ramsey, of Trinity College, Cambridge, for assistance both with the translation and in the preparation of the book for the press.*

C. K. O.

INTRODUCTION

By BERTRAND RUSSELL

MR WITTGENSTEIN'S *Tractatus Logico-Philosophicus*, whether or not it prove to give the ultimate truth on the matters with which it deals, certainly deserves, by its breadth and scope and profundity, to be considered an important event in the philosophical world. Starting from the principles of Symbolism and the relations which are necessary between words and things in any language, it applies the result of this inquiry to various departments of traditional philosophy, showing in each case how traditional philosophy and traditional solutions arise out of ignorance of the principles of Symbolism and out of misuse of language.

The logical structure of propositions and the nature of logical inference are first dealt with. Thence we pass successively to Theory of Knowledge, Principles of Physics, Ethics, and finally the Mystical (*das Mystische*).

In order to understand Mr Wittgenstein's book, it is necessary to realize what is the problem with which he is concerned. In the part of his theory which deals with Symbolism he is concerned with the conditions which would have to be fulfilled by a logically perfect language. There are various problems as regards language. First, there is the problem what actually occurs in our minds when we use language with the intention of meaning something by it; this problem belongs to psychology. Secondly, there is the problem as to what is the relation subsisting between thoughts, words, or sentences, and that which they refer to or mean; this problem belongs to epistemology. Thirdly, there is the problem of using sentences so as to convey truth rather than falsehood;

this belongs to the special sciences dealing with the subject-matter of the sentences in question. Fourthly, there is the question : what relation must one fact (such as a sentence) have to another in order to be *capable* of being a symbol for that other? This last is a logical question, and is the one with which Mr Wittgenstein is concerned. He is concerned with the conditions for *accurate* Symbolism, *i.e.* for Symbolism in which a sentence "means" something quite definite. In practice, language is always more or less vague, so that what we assert is never quite precise. Thus, logic has two problems to deal with in regard to Symbolism : (1) the conditions for sense rather than nonsense in combinations of symbols ; (2) the conditions for uniqueness of meaning or reference in symbols or combinations of symbols. A logically perfect language has rules of syntax which prevent nonsense, and has single symbols which always have a definite and unique meaning. Mr Wittgenstein is concerned with the conditions for a logically perfect language—not that any language is logically perfect, or that we believe ourselves capable, here and now, of constructing a logically perfect language, but that the whole function of language is to have meaning, and it only fulfils this function in proportion as it approaches to the ideal language which we postulate.

The essential business of language is to assert or deny facts. Given the syntax of a language, the meaning of a sentence is determinate as soon as the meaning of the component words is known. In order that a certain sentence should assert a certain fact there must, however the language may be constructed, be something in common between the structure of the sentence and the structure of the fact. This is perhaps the most fundamental thesis of Mr Wittgenstein's theory. That which has to be in common between the sentence and the fact cannot, so he contends, be itself in turn *said* in language. It can, in his phraseology, only be *shown*, not said, for whatever we may say will still need to have the same structure.

8

INTRODUCTION

The first requisite of an ideal language would be that there should be one name for every simple, and never the same name for two different simples. A name is a simple symbol in the sense that it has no parts which are themselves symbols. In a logically perfect language nothing that is not simple will have a simple symbol. The symbol for the whole will be a "complex," containing the symbols for the parts. In speaking of a "complex" we are, as will appear later, sinning against the rules of philosophical grammar, but this is unavoidable at the outset. "Most propositions and questions that have been written about philosophical matters are not false but senseless. We cannot, therefore, answer questions of this kind at all, but only state their senselessness. Most questions and propositions of the philosopher result from the fact that we do not understand the logic of our language. They are of the same kind as the question whether the Good is more or less identical than the Beautiful" (4.003). What is complex in the world is a fact. Facts which are not compounded of other facts are what Mr Wittgenstein calls *Sachverhalte*, whereas a fact which may consist of two or more facts is called a *Tatsache*: thus, for example, "Socrates is wise" is a *Sachverhalt*, as well as a *Tatsache*, whereas "Socrates is wise and Plato is his pupil" is a *Tatsache* but not a *Sachverhalt*.

He compares linguistic expression to projection in geometry. A geometrical figure may be projected in many ways: each of these ways corresponds to a different language, but the projective properties of the original figure remain unchanged whichever of these ways may be adopted. These projective properties correspond to that which in his theory the proposition and the fact must have in common, if the proposition is to assert the fact.

In certain elementary ways this is, of course, obvious. It is impossible, for example, to make a statement about two men (assuming for the moment that the men may be treated as simples), without employing two names, and

if you are going to assert a relation between the two men
it will be necessary that the sentence in which you make
the assertion shall establish a relation between the two
names. If we say "Plato loves Socrates," the word
"loves" which occurs between the word "Plato" and the
word "Socrates" establishes a certain relation between
these two words, and it is owing to this fact that our
sentence is able to assert a relation between the person's
name by the words "Plato" and "Socrates." "We must
not say, the complex sign '$a R b$' says 'a stands in a
certain relation R to b'; but we must say, that 'a'
stands in a certain relation to 'b' says *that a R b*"
(3.1432).

Mr Wittgenstein begins his theory of Symbolism with
the statement (2.1): "We make to ourselves pictures of
facts." A picture, he says, is a model of the reality, and
to the objects in the reality correspond the elements of
the picture: the picture itself is a fact. The fact that
things have a certain relation to each other is represented
by the fact that in the picture its elements have a certain
relation to one another. "In the picture and the pictured
there must be something identical in order that the one
can be a picture of the other at all. What the picture
must have in common with reality in order to be able
to represent it after its manner—rightly or falsely—is its
form of representation" (2.161, 2.17).

We speak of a logical picture of a reality when we
wish to imply only so much resemblance as is essential to
its being a picture in any sense, that is to say, when we
wish to imply no more than identity of logical form.
The logical picture of a fact, he says, is a *Gedanke*. A
picture can correspond or not correspond with the fact and
be accordingly true or false, but in both cases it shares the
logical form with the fact. The sense in which he speaks of
pictures is illustrated by his statement: "The gramophone
record, the musical thought, the score, the waves of sound,
all stand to one another in that pictorial internal relation
which holds between language and the world. To all of

them the logical structure is common. (Like the two youths, their two horses and their lilies in the story. They are all in a certain sense one)" (4.014). The possibility of a proposition representing a fact rests upon the fact that in it objects are represented by signs. The so-called logical "constants" are not represented by signs, but are themselves present in the proposition as in the fact. The proposition and the fact must exhibit the same logical "manifold," and this cannot be itself represented since it has to be in common between the fact and the picture. Mr Wittgenstein maintains that everything properly philosophical belongs to what can only be shown, to what is in common between a fact and its logical picture. It results from this view that nothing correct can be said in philosophy. Every philosophical proposition is bad grammar, and the best that we can hope to achieve by philosophical discussion is to lead people to see that philosophical discussion is a mistake. "Philosophy is not one of the natural sciences. (The word 'philosophy' must mean something which stands above or below, but not beside the natural sciences.) The object of philosophy is the logical clarification of thoughts. Philosophy is not a theory but an activity. A philosophical work consists essentially of elucidations. The result of philosophy is not a number of 'philosophical propositions,' but to make propositions clear. Philosophy should make clear and delimit sharply the thoughts which otherwise are, as it were, opaque and blurred" (4.111 and 4.112). In accordance with this principle the things that have to be said in leading the reader to understand Mr Wittgenstein's theory are all of them things which that theory itself condemns as meaningless. With this proviso we will endeavour to convey the picture of the world which seems to underlie his system.

The world consists of facts: facts cannot strictly speaking be defined, but we can explain what we mean by saying that facts are what make propositions true, or false. Facts may contain parts which are facts or may

contain no such parts ; for example : " Socrates was a wise Athenian," consists of the two facts, " Socrates was wise," and " Socrates was an Athenian." A fact which has no parts that are facts is called by Mr Wittgenstein a *Sachverhalt.* This is the same thing that he calls an atomic fact. An atomic fact, although it contains no parts that are facts, nevertheless does contain parts. If we may regard " Socrates is wise " as an atomic fact we perceive that it contains the constituents " Socrates " and " wise." If an atomic fact is analysed as fully as possibly (theoretical, not practical possibility is meant) the constituents finally reached may be called " simples " or " objects." It is not contended by Wittgenstein that we can actually isolate the simple or have empirical knowledge of it. It is a logical necessity demanded by theory, like an electron. His ground for maintaining that there must be simples is that every complex presupposes a fact. It is not necessarily assumed that the complexity of facts is finite ; even if every fact consisted of an infinite number of atomic facts and if every atomic fact consisted of an infinite number of objects there would still be objects and atomic facts (4.2211). The assertion that there is a certain complex reduces to the assertion that its constituents are related in a certain way, which is the assertion of a *fact :* thus if we give a name to the complex the name only has meaning in virtue of the truth of a certain proposition, namely the proposition asserting the relatedness of the constituents of the complex. Thus the naming of complexes presupposes propositions, while propositions presupposes the naming of simples. In this way the naming of simples is shown to be what is logically first in logic.

The world is fully described if all atomic facts are known, together with the fact that these are all of them. The world is not described by merely naming all the objects in it ; it is necessary also to know the atomic facts of which these objects are constituents. Given this total of atomic facts, every true proposition, however complex,

can theoretically be inferred. A proposition (true or false) asserting an atomic fact is called an atomic proposition. All atomic propositions are logically independent of each other. No atomic proposition implies any other or is inconsistent with any other. Thus the whole business of logical inference is concerned with propositions which are not atomic. Such propositions may be called molecular.

Wittgenstein's theory of molecular propositions turns upon his theory of the construction of truth-functions.

A truth-function of a proposition p is a proposition containing p and such that its truth or falsehood depends only upon the truth or falsehood of p, and similarly a truth-function of several propositions p, q, r . . . is one containing p, q, r . . . and such that its truth or falsehood depends only upon the truth or falsehood of p, q, r . . . It might seem at first sight as though there were other functions of propositions besides truth-functions ; such, for example, would be " A believes p," for in general A will believe some true propositions and some false ones : unless he is an exceptionally gifted individual, we cannot infer that p is true from the fact that he believes it or that p is false from the fact that he does not believe it. Other apparent exceptions would be such as "p is a very complex proposition " or "p is a proposition about Socrates." Mr Wittgenstein maintains, however, for reasons which will appear presently, that such exceptions are only apparent, and that every function of a proposition is really a truth-function. It follows that if we can define truth-functions generally, we can obtain a general definition of all propositions in terms of the original set of atomic propositions. This Wittgenstein proceeds to do.

It has been shown by Dr Sheffer (*Trans. Am. Math. Soc.*, Vol. XIV. pp. 481-488) that all truth-functions of a given set of propositions can be constructed out of either of the two functions "not-p or not-q" or "not-p and not-q." Wittgenstein makes use of the latter, assuming a know-

ledge of Dr Sheffer's work. The manner in which other truth-functions are constructed out of "not-p and not-q" is easy to see. "Not-p and not-p" is equivalent to "not-p," hence we obtain a definition of negation in terms of our primitive function : hence we can define "p or q," since this is the negation of "not-p and not-q," *i.e.* of our primitive function. The development of other truth-functions out of "not-p" and "p or q" is given in detail at the beginning of *Principia Mathematica*. This gives all that is wanted when the propositions which are arguments to our truth-function are given by enumeration. Wittgenstein, however, by a very interesting analysis succeeds in extending the process to general propositions, *i.e.* to cases where the propositions which are arguments to our truth-function are not given by enumeration but are given as all those satisfying some condition. For example, let fx be a propositional function (*i.e.* a function whose values are propositions), such as "x is human"—then the various values of fx form a set of propositions. We may extend the idea "not-p and not-q" so as to apply to simultaneous denial of all the propositions which are values of fx. In this way we arrive at the proposition which is ordinarily represented in mathematical logic by the words "fx is false for all values of x." The negation of this would be the proposition "there is at least one x for which fx is true" which is represented by "$(\exists x) . fx$." If we had started with not-fx instead of fx we should have arrived at the proposition "fx is true for all values of x" which is represented by "$(x) . fx$." Wittgenstein's method of dealing with general propositions [*i.e.* "$(x) . fx$" and "$(\exists x) . fx$"] differs from previous methods by the fact that the generality comes only in specifying the set of propositions concerned, and when this has been done the building up of truth-functions proceeds exactly as it would in the case of a finite number of enumerated arguments $p, q, r. \ldots$

Mr Wittgenstein's explanation of his symbolism at this point is not quite fully given in the text. The symbol

he uses is $(\bar{p}, \bar{\xi}, \bar{N}(\bar{\xi}))$. The following is the explanation of this symbol :

$\bar{p}$ stands for all atomic propositions.

$\bar{\xi}$ stands for any set of propositions.

$\bar{N}(\bar{\xi})$ stands for the negation of all the propositions making up $\bar{\xi}$.

The whole symbol $(\bar{p}, \bar{\xi}, \bar{N}(\bar{\xi}))$ means whatever can be obtained by taking any selection of atomic propositions, negating them all, then taking any selection of the set of propositions now obtained, together with any of the originals—and so on indefinitely. This is, he says, the general truth-function and also the general form of proposition. What is meant is somewhat less complicated than it sounds. The symbol is intended to describe a process by the help of which, given the atomic propositions, all others can be manufactured. The process depends upon :

(*a*) Sheffer's proof that all truth-functions can be obtained out of simultaneous negation, *i.e.* out of " not-*p* and not-*q* ";

(*b*) Mr Wittgenstein's theory of the derivation of general propositions from conjunctions and disjunctions ;

(*c*) The assertion that a proposition can only occur in another proposition as argument to a truth - function. Given these three foundations, it follows that all propositions which are not atomic can be derived from such as are, by a uniform process, and it is this process which is indicated by Mr Wittgenstein's symbol.

From this uniform method of construction we arrive at an amazing simplification of the theory of inference, as well as a definition of the sort of propositions that belong to logic. The method of generation which has just been described, enables Wittgenstein to say that all propositions can be constructed in the above manner from atomic propositions, and in this way the totality of propositions is defined. (The apparent exceptions which we mentioned above are dealt with in a manner which we

shall consider later.) Wittgenstein is enabled to assert that propositions are all that follows from the totality of atomic propositions (together with the fact that it is the totality of them); that a proposition is always a truth-function of atomic propositions; and that if p follows from q the meaning of p is contained in the meaning of q, from which of course it results that nothing can be deduced from an atomic proposition. All the propositions of logic, he maintains, are tautologies, such, for example, as "p or not p."

The fact that nothing can be deduced from an atomic proposition has interesting applications, for example, to causality. There cannot, in Wittgenstein's logic, be any such thing as a causal nexus. "The events of the future," he says, "*cannot* be inferred from those of the present. Superstition is the belief in the causal nexus." That the sun will rise to-morrow is a hypothesis. We do not in fact know whether it will rise, since there is no compulsion according to which one thing must happen because another happens.

Let us now take up another subject—that of names. In Wittgenstein's theoretical logical language, names are only given to simples. We do not give two names to one thing, or one name to two things. There is no way whatever, according to him, by which we can describe the totality of things that can be named, in other words, the totality of what there is in the world. In order to be able to do this we should have to know of some property which must belong to every thing by a logical necessity. It has been sought to find such a property in self-identity, but the conception of identity is subjected by Wittgenstein to a destructive criticism from which there seems no escape. The definition of identity by means of the identity of indiscernibles is rejected, because the identity of indiscernibles appears to be not a logically necessary principle. According to this principle x is identical with y if every property of x is a property of y, but it would, after all, be logically possible for two things to have exactly the same properties.

If this does not in fact happen that is an accidental characteristic of the world, not a logically necessary characteristic, and accidental characteristics of the world must, of course, not be admitted into the structure of logic. Mr Wittgenstein accordingly banishes identity and adopts the convention that different letters are to mean different things. In practice, identity is needed as between a name and a description or between two descriptions. It is needed for such propositions as "Socrates is the philosopher who drank the hemlock," or "The even prime is the next number after 1." For such uses of identity it is easy to provide on Wittgenstein's system.

The rejection of identity removes one method of speaking of the totality of things, and it will be found that any other method that may be suggested is equally fallacious: so, at least, Wittgenstein contends and, I think, rightly. This amounts to saying that "object" is a pseudo-concept. To say "x is an object" is to say nothing. It follows from this that we cannot make such statements as "there are more than three objects in the world," or "there are an infinite number of objects in the world." Objects can only be mentioned in connexion with some definite property. We can say "there are more than three objects which are human," or "there are more than three objects which are red," for in these statements the word object can be replaced by a variable in the language of logic, the variable being one which satisfies in the first case the function "x is human"; in the second the function "x is red." But when we attempt to say "there are more than three objects," this substitution of the variable for the word "object" becomes impossible, and the proposition is therefore seen to be meaningless.

We here touch one instance of Wittgenstein's fundamental thesis, that it is impossible to say anything about the world as a whole, and that whatever can be said has to be about bounded portions of the world. This view may have been originally suggested by notation, and if so, that is much in its favour, for a good notation has

a subtlety and suggestiveness which at times make it seem almost like a live teacher. Notational irregularities are often the first sign of philosophical errors, and a perfect notation would be a substitute for thought. But although notation may have first suggested to Mr Wittgenstein the limitation of logic to things within the world as opposed to the world as a whole, yet the view, once suggested, is seen to have much else to recommend it. Whether it is ultimately true I do not, for my part, profess to know. In this Introduction I am concerned to expound it, not to pronounce upon it. According to this view we could only say things about the world as a whole if we could get outside the world, if, that is to say, it ceased to be for us the whole world. Our world may be bounded for some superior being who can survey it from above, but for us, however finite it may be, it cannot have a boundary, since it has nothing outside it. Wittgenstein uses, as an analogy, the field of vision. Our field of vision does not, for us, have a visual boundary, just because there is nothing outside it, and in like manner our logical world has no logical boundary because our logic knows of nothing outside it. These considerations lead him to a somewhat curious discussion of Solipsism. Logic, he says, fills the world. The boundaries of the world are also its boundaries. In logic, therefore, we cannot say, there is this and this in the world, but not that, for to say so would apparently presuppose that we exclude certain possibilities, and this cannot be the case, since it would require that logic should go beyond the boundaries of the world as if it could contemplate these boundaries from the other side also. What we cannot think we cannot think, therefore we also cannot say what we cannot think.

This, he says, gives the key to Solipsism. What Solipsism intends is quite correct, but this cannot be said, it can only be shown. That the world is *my* world appears in the fact that the boundaries of language (the only language I understand) indicate the boundaries of

my world. The metaphysical subject does not belong to the world but is a boundary of the world.

We must take up next the question of molecular propositions which are at first sight not truth-functions, of the propositions that they contain, such, for example, as "A believes p."

Wittgenstein introduces this subject in the statement of his position, namely, that all molecular functions are truth-functions. He says (5.54): "In the general propositional form, propositions occur in a proposition only as bases of truth-operations." At first sight, he goes on to explain, it seems as if a proposition could also occur in other ways, e.g. "A believes p." Here it seems superficially as if the proposition p stood in a sort of relation to the object A. "But it is clear that 'A believes that p,' 'A thinks p,' 'A says p' are of the form 'p says p'; and here we have no co-ordination of a fact and an object, but a co-ordination of facts by means of a co-ordination of their objects" (5.542).

What Mr Wittgenstein says here is said so shortly that its point is not likely to be clear to those who have not in mind the controversies with which he is concerned. The theory with which he is disagreeing will be found in my articles on the nature of truth and falsehood in *Philosophical Essays* and *Proceedings of the Aristotelian Society*, 1906-7. The problem at issue is the problem of the logical form of belief, *i.e.* what is the schema representing what occurs when a man believes. Of course, the problem applies not only to belief, but also to a host of other mental phenomena which may be called propositional attitudes: doubting, considering, desiring, etc. In all these cases it seems natural to express the phenomenon in the form "A doubts p," "A desires p," etc., which makes it appear as though we were dealing with a relation between a person and a proposition. This cannot, of course, be the ultimate analysis, since persons are fictions and so are propositions, except in the sense in which they are facts on their own account. A proposition, considered

as a fact on its own account, may be a set of words which a man says over to himself, or a complex image, or train of images passing through his mind, or a set of incipient bodily movements. It may be any one of innumerable different things. The proposition as a fact on its own account, for example the actual set of words the man pronounces to himself, is not relevant to logic. What is relevant to logic is that common element among all these facts, which enables him, as we say, to *mean* the fact which the proposition asserts. To psychology, of course, more is relevant; for a symbol does not mean what it symbolizes in virtue of a logical relation alone, but in virtue also of a psychological relation of intention, or association, or what-not. The psychological part of meaning, however, does not concern the logician. What does concern him in this problem of belief is the logical schema. It is clear that, when a person believes a proposition, the person, considered as a metaphysical subject, does not have to be assumed in order to explain what is happening. What has to be explained is the relation between the set of words which is the proposition considered as a fact on its own account, and the "objective" fact which makes the proposition true or false. This reduces ultimately to the question of the meaning of propositions, that is to say, the meaning of propositions is the only non-psychological portion of the problem involved in the analysis of belief. This problem is simply one of a relation of two facts, namely, the relation between the series of words used by the believer and the fact which makes these words true or false. The series of words is a fact just as much as what makes it true or false is a fact. The relation between these two facts is not unanalysable, since the meaning of a proposition results from the meaning of its constituent words. The meaning of the series of words which is a proposition is a function of the meanings of the separate words. Accordingly, the proposition as a whole does not really enter into what has to be explained in explaining the meaning of a proposition. It would

perhaps help to suggest the point of view which I am trying to indicate, to say that in the cases we have been considering the proposition occurs as a fact, not as a proposition. Such a statement, however, must not be taken too literally. The real point is that in believing, desiring, etc., what is logically fundamental is the relation of a proposition *considered as a fact*, to the fact which makes it true or false, and that this relation of two facts is reducible to a relation of their constituents. Thus the proposition does not occur at all in the same sense in which it occurs in a truth-function.

There are some respects, in which, as it seems to me, Mr Wittgenstein's theory stands in need of greater technical development. This applies in particular to his theory of number (6.02 ff.) which, as it stands, is only capable of dealing with finite numbers. No logic can be considered adequate until it has been shown to be capable of dealing with transfinite numbers. I do not think there is anything in Mr Wittgenstein's system to make it impossible for him to fill this lacuna.

More interesting than such questions of comparative detail is Mr Wittgenstein's attitude towards the mystical. His attitude upon this grows naturally out of his doctrine in pure logic, according to which the logical proposition is a picture (true or false) of the fact, and has in common with the fact a certain structure. It is this common structure which makes it capable of being a picture of the fact, but the structure cannot itself be put into words, since it is a structure *of* words, as well as of the facts to which they refer. Everything, therefore, which is involved in the very idea of the expressiveness of language must remain incapable of being expressed in language, and is, therefore, inexpressible in a perfectly precise sense. This inexpressible contains, according to Mr Wittgenstein, the whole of logic and philosophy. The right method of teaching philosophy, he says, would be to confine oneself to propositions of the sciences, stated with all possible clearness and exactness, leaving philosophical assertions

to the learner, and proving to him, whenever he made them, that they are meaningless. It is true that the fate of Socrates might befall a man who attempted this method of teaching, but we are not to be deterred by that fear, if it is the only right method. It is not this that causes some hesitation in accepting Mr Wittgenstein's position, in spite of the very powerful arguments which he brings to its support. What causes hesitation is the fact that, after all, Mr Wittgenstein manages to say a good deal about what cannot be said, thus suggesting to the sceptical reader that possibly there may be some loophole through a hierarchy of languages, or by some other exit. The whole subject of ethics, for example, is placed by Mr Wittgenstein in the mystical, inexpressible region. Nevertheless he is capable of conveying his ethical opinions. His defence would be that what he calls the mystical can be shown, although it cannot be said. It may be that this defence is adequate, but, for my part, I confess that it leaves me with a certain sense of intellectual discomfort.

There is one purely logical problem in regard to which these difficulties are peculiarly acute. I mean the problem of generality. In the theory of generality it is necessary to consider all propositions of the form fx where fx is a given propositional function. This belongs to the part of logic which can be expressed, according to Mr Wittgenstein's system. But the totality of possible values of x which might seem to be involved in the totality of propositions of the form fx is not admitted by Mr Wittgenstein among the things that can be spoken of, for this is no other than the totality of things in the world, and thus involves the attempt to conceive the world as a whole; "the feeling of the world as a bounded whole is the mystical"; hence the totality of the values of x is mystical (6.45). This is expressly argued when Mr Wittgenstein denies that we can make propositions as to how many things there are in the world, as for example, that there are more than three.

INTRODUCTION

These difficulties suggest to my mind some such possibility as this: that every language has, as Mr Wittgenstein says, a structure concerning which, *in the language*, nothing can be said, but that there may be another language dealing with the structure of the first language, and having itself a new structure, and that to this hierarchy of languages there may be no limit. Mr Wittgenstein would of course reply that his whole theory is applicable unchanged to the totality of such languages. The only retort would be to deny that there is any such totality. The totalities concerning which Mr Wittgenstein holds that it is impossible to speak logically are nevertheless thought by him to exist, and are the subject-matter of his mysticism. The totality resulting from our hierarchy would be not merely logically inexpressible, but a fiction, a mere delusion, and in this way the supposed sphere of the mystical would be abolished. Such an hypothesis is very difficult, and I can see objections to it which at the moment I do not know how to answer. Yet I do not see how any easier hypothesis can escape from Mr Wittgenstein's conclusions. Even if this very difficult hypothesis should prove tenable, it would leave untouched a very large part of Mr Wittgenstein's theory, though possibly not the part upon which he himself would wish to lay most stress. As one with a long experience of the difficulties of logic and of the deceptiveness of theories which seem irrefutable, I find myself unable to be sure of the rightness of a theory, merely on the ground that I cannot see any point on which it is wrong. But to have constructed a theory of logic which is not at any point obviously wrong is to have achieved a work of extraordinary difficulty and importance. This merit, in my opinion, belongs to Mr Wittgenstein's book, and makes it one which no serious philosopher can afford to neglect.

BERTRAND RUSSELL.

May 1922.

Tractatus Logico-Philosophicus

Motto: . . . und alles, was man weiss, nicht bloss rauschen
und brausen gehört hat, lässt sich in drei Worten sagen.
KÜRNBERGER.

Logisch-Philosophische Abhandlung

VORWORT

Dieses Buch wird vielleicht nur der verstehen, der die Gedanken, die darin ausgedrückt sind—oder doch ähnliche Gedanken—schon selbst einmal gedacht hat.— Es ist also kein Lehrbuch.—Sein Zweck wäre erreicht, wenn es Einem, der es mit Verständnis liest Vergnügen bereitete.

Das Buch behandelt die philosophischen Probleme und zeigt—wie ich glaube—dass die Fragestellung dieser Probleme auf dem Missverständnis der Logik unserer Sprache beruht. Man könnte den ganzen Sinn des Buches etwa in die Worte fassen: Was sich überhaupt sagen lässt, lässt sich klar sagen; und wovon man nicht reden kann, darüber muss man schweigen.

Das Buch will also dem Denken eine Grenze ziehen, oder vielmehr—nicht dem Denken, sondern dem Ausdruck der Gedanken: Denn um dem Denken eine Grenze zu ziehen, müssten wir beide Seiten dieser Grenze denken können (wir müssten also denken können, was sich nicht denken lässt).

Die Grenze wird also nur in der Sprache gezogen werden können und was jenseits der Grenze liegt, wird einfach Unsinn sein.

Wieweit meine Bestrebungen mit denen anderer Philosophen zusammenfallen, will ich nicht beurteilen. Ja, was ich hier geschrieben habe macht im Einzelnen überhaupt nicht den Anspruch auf Neuheit; und darum gebe ich auch keine Quellen an, weil es mir gleichgültig ist, ob das was ich gedacht habe, vor mir schon ein anderer gedacht hat.

Tractatus Logico-Philosophicus

PREFACE

This book will perhaps only be understood by those who have themselves already thought the thoughts which are expressed in it—or similar thoughts. It is therefore not a text-book. Its object would be attained if it afforded pleasure to one who read it with understanding.

The book deals with the problems of philosophy and shows, as I believe, that the method of formulating these problems rests on the misunderstanding of the logic of our language. Its whole meaning could be summed up somewhat as follows: What can be said at all can be said clearly; and whereof one cannot speak thereof one must be silent.

The book will, therefore, draw a limit to thinking, or rather—not to thinking, but to the expression of thoughts; for, in order to draw a limit to thinking we should have to be able to think both sides of this limit (we should therefore have to be able to think what cannot be thought).

The limit can, therefore, only be drawn in language and what lies on the other side of the limit will be simply nonsense.

How far my efforts agree with those of other philosophers I will not decide. Indeed what I have here written makes no claim to novelty in points of detail; and therefore I give no sources, because it is indifferent to me whether what I have thought has already been thought before me by another.

LOGISCH-PHILOSOPHISCHE ABHANDLUNG

Nur das will ich erwähnen, dass ich den grossartigen Werken Freges und den Arbeiten meines Freundes Herrn Bertrand Russell einen grossen Teil der Anregung zu meinen Gedanken schulde.

Wenn diese Arbeit einen Wert hat, so besteht er in Zweierlei. Erstens darin, dass in ihr Gedanken ausgedrückt sind, und dieser Wert wird umso grösser sein, je besser die Gedanken ausgedrückt sind. Je mehr der Nagel auf den Kopf getroffen ist.—Hier bin ich mir bewusst, weit hinter dem Möglichen zurückgeblieben zu sein. Einfach darum, weil meine Kraft zur Bewältigung der Aufgabe zu gering ist.—Mögen andere kommen und es besser machen.

Dagegen scheint mir die W a h r h e i t der hier mitgeteilten Gedanken unantastbar und definitiv. Ich bin also der Meinung, die Probleme im Wesentlichen endgültig gelöst zu haben. Und wenn ich mich hierin nicht irre, so besteht nun der Wert dieser Arbeit zweitens darin, dass sie zeigt, wie wenig damit getan ist, dass diese Probleme gelöst sind.

L. W.

Wien, 1918.

28

I will only mention that to the great works of Frege and the writings of my friend Bertrand Russell I owe in large measure the stimulation of my thoughts.

If this work has a value it consists in two things. First that in it thoughts are expressed, and this value will be the greater the better the thoughts are expressed. The more the nail has been hit on the head.—Here I am conscious that I have fallen far short of the possible. Simply because my powers are insufficient to cope with the task.—May others come and do it better.

On the other hand the *truth* of the thoughts communicated here seems to me unassailable and definitive. I am, therefore, of the opinion that the problems have in essentials been finally solved. And if I am not mistaken in this, then the value of this work secondly consists in the fact that it shows how little has been done when these problems have been solved.

1*	Die Welt ist alles, was der Fall ist.
1.1	Die Welt ist die Gesamtheit der Tatsachen, nicht der Dinge.
1.11	Die Welt ist durch die Tatsachen bestimmt und dadurch, dass es a l l e Tatsachen sind.
1.12	Denn, die Gesamtheit der Tatsachen bestimmt, was der Fall ist und auch, was alles nicht der Fall ist.
1.13	Die Tatsachen im logischen Raum sind die Welt.
1.2	Die Welt zerfällt in Tatsachen.
1.21	Eines kann der Fall sein oder nicht der Fall sein und alles übrige gleich bleiben.
2	Was der Fall ist, die Tatsache, ist das Bestehen von Sachverhalten.
2.01	Der Sachverhalt ist eine Verbindung von Gegenständen. (Sachen, Dingen.)
2.011	Es ist dem Ding wesentlich, der Bestandteil eines Sachverhaltes sein zu können.
2.012	In der Logik ist nichts zufällig : Wenn das Ding im Sachverhalt vorkommen k a n n, so muss die Möglichkeit des Sachverhaltes im Ding bereits präjudiziert sein.
2.0121	Es erschiene gleichsam als Zufall, wenn dem Ding, das allein für sich bestehen könnte, nachträglich eine Sachlage passen würde.
	Wenn die Dinge in Sachverhalten vorkommen können, so muss dies schon in ihnen liegen.
	(Etwas Logisches kann nicht nur-möglich sein. Die Logik handelt von jeder Möglichkeit und alle Möglichkeiten sind ihre Tatsachen.)

* Die Decimalzahlen als Nummern der einzelnen Sätze deuten das logische Gewicht der Sätze an, den Nachdruck, der auf ihnen in meiner Darstellung liegt, Die Sätze n. 1, n. 2, n. 3, etc., sind Bemerkungen zum Sätze No. n ; die Sätze n.m1, n.m2, etc. Bemerkungen zum Satze No. n.m ; und so weiter.

1	The world is everything that is the case.*
1.1	The world is the totality of facts, not of things.
1.11	The world is determined by the facts, and by these being *all* the facts.
1.12	For the totality of facts determines both what is the case, and also all that is not the case.
1.13	The facts in logical space are the world.
1.2	The world divides into facts.
1.21	Any one can either be the case or not be the case, and everything else remain the same.
2	What is the case, the fact, is the existence of atomic facts.
2.01	An atomic fact is a combination of objects (entities, things).
2.011	It is essential to a thing that it can be a constituent part of an atomic fact.
2.012	In logic nothing is accidental : if a thing *can* occur in an atomic fact the possibility of that atomic fact must already be prejudged in the thing.
2.0121	It would, so to speak, appear as an accident, when to a thing that could exist alone on its own account, subsequently a state of affairs could be made to fit.
	If things can occur in atomic facts, this possibility must already lie in them.
	(A logical entity cannot be merely possible. Logic treats of every possibility, and all possibilities are its facts.)

* The decimal figures as numbers of the separate propositions indicate the logical importance of the propositions, the emphasis laid upon them in my exposition. The propositions *n*.1, *n*.2, *n*.3, etc., are comments on proposition No. *n* ; the propositions *n*.*m*1, *n*.*m*2, etc., are comments on the proposition No. *n*.*m* ; and so on.

Wie wir uns räumliche Gegenstände überhaupt nicht ausserhalb des Raumes, zeitliche nicht ausserhalb der Zeit denken können, so können wir uns k e i n e n Gegenstand ausserhalb der Möglichkeit seiner Verbindung mit anderen denken.

Wenn ich mir den Gegenstand im Verbande des Sachverhalts denken kann, so kann ich ihn nicht ausserhalb der M ö g l i c h k e i t dieses Verbandes denken.

2.0122 Das Ding ist selbständig, insofern es in allen m ö g l i c h e n Sachlagen vorkommen kann, aber diese Form der Selbständigkeit ist eine Form des Zusammenhangs mit dem Sachverhalt, eine Form der Unselbständigkeit. (Es ist unmöglich, dass Worte in zwei verschiedenen Weisen auftreten, allein und im Satz.)

2.0123 Wenn ich den Gegenstand kenne, so kenne ich auch sämtliche Möglichkeiten seines Vorkommens in Sachverhalten.

(Jede solche Möglichkeit muss in der Natur des Gegenstandes liegen.)

Es kann nicht nachträglich eine neue Möglichkeit gefunden werden.

2.01231 Um einen Gegenstand zu kennen, muss ich zwar nicht seine externen — aber ich muss alle seine internen Eigenschaften kennen.

2.0124 Sind alle Gegenstände gegeben, so sind damit auch alle m ö g l i c h e n Sachverhalte gegeben.

2.013 Jedes Ding ist, gleichsam, in einem Raume möglicher Sachverhalte. Diesen Raum kann ich mir leer denken, nicht aber das Ding ohne den Raum.

2.0131 Der räumliche Gegenstand muss im unendlichen Raume liegen. (Der Raumpunkt ist eine Argumentstelle.)

Der Fleck im Gesichtsfeld muss zwar nicht rot sein, aber eine Farbe muss er haben : er hat sozusagen den Farbenraum um sich. Der Ton muss

Just as we cannot think of spatial objects at all apart from space, or temporal objects apart from time, so we cannot think of *any* object apart from the possibility of its connexion with other things.

If I can think of an object in the context of an atomic fact, I cannot think of it apart from the *possibility* of this context.

2.0122 The thing is independent, in so far as it can occur in all *possible* circumstances, but this form of independence is a form of connexion with the atomic fact, a form of dependence. (It is impossible for words to occur in two different ways, alone and in the proposition.)

2.0123 If I know an object, then I also know all the possibilities of its occurrence in atomic facts.

(Every such possibility must lie in the nature of the object.)

A new possibility cannot subsequently be found.

2.01231 In order to know an object, I must know not its external but all its internal qualities.

2.0124 If all objects are given, then thereby are all *possible* atomic facts also given.

2.013 Every thing is, as it were, in a space of possible atomic facts. I can think of this space as empty, but not of the thing without the space.

2.0131 A spatial object must lie in infinite space. (A point in space is an argument place.)

A speck in a visual field need not be red, but it must have a colour; it has, so to speak, a colour space round it. A tone must have *a*

e i n e Höhe haben, der Gegenstand des Tastsinnes
e i n e Härte usw.

2.014 Die Gegenstände enthalten die Möglichkeit aller Sachlagen.

2.0141 Die Möglichkeit seines Vorkommens in Sachverhalten, ist die Form des Gegenstandes.

2.02 Der Gegenstand ist einfach.

2.0201 Jede Aussage über Komplexe lässt sich in eine Aussage über deren Bestandteile und in diejenigen Sätze zerlegen, welche die Komplexe vollständig beschreiben.

2.021 Die Gegenstände bilden die Substanz der Welt. Darum können sie nicht zusammengesetzt sein.

2.0211 Hätte die Welt keine Substanz, so würde, ob ein Satz Sinn hat, davon abhängen, ob ein anderer Satz wahr ist.

2.0212 Es wäre dann unmöglich, ein Bild der Welt (wahr oder falsch) zu entwerfen.

2.022 Es ist offenbar, dass auch eine von der wirklichen noch so verschieden gedachte Welt Etwas— eine Form—mit der wirklichen gemein haben muss.

2.023 Diese feste Form besteht eben aus den Gegenständen.

2.0231 Die Substanz der Welt k a n n nur eine Form und keine materiellen Eigenschaften bestimmen. Denn diese werden erst durch die Sätze dargestellt—erst durch die Konfiguration der Gegenstände gebildet.

2.0232 Beiläufig gesprochen : Die Gegenstände sind farblos.

2.0233 Zwei Gegenstände von der gleichen logischen Form sind—abgesehen von ihren externen Eigenschaften—von einander nur dadurch unterschieden, dass sie verschieden sind.

2.02331 Entweder ein Ding hat Eigenschaften, die kein anderes hat, dann kann man es ohneweiteres durch eine Beschreibung aus den anderen herausheben, und darauf hinweisen ; oder aber, es gibt mehrere Dinge, die ihre sämtlichen Eigenschaften gemein-

pitch, the object of the sense of touch *a* hardness, etc.

2.014 Objects contain the possibility of all states of affairs.

2.0141 The possibility of its occurrence in atomic facts is the form of the object.

2.02 The object is simple.

2.0201 Every statement about complexes can be analysed into a statement about their constituent parts, and into those propositions which completely describe the complexes.

2.021 Objects form the substance of the world. Therefore they cannot be compound.

2.0211 If the world had no substance, then whether a proposition had sense would depend on whether another proposition was true.

2.0212 It would then be impossible to form a picture of the world (true or false).

2.022 It is clear that however different from the real one an imagined world may be, it must have something—a form—in common with the real world.

2.023 This fixed form consists of the objects.

2.0231 The substance of the world *can* only determine a form and not any material properties. For these are first presented by the propositions—first formed by the configuration of the objects.

2.0232 Roughly speaking : objects are colourless.

2.0233 Two objects of the same logical form are—apart from their external properties—only differentiated from one another in that they are different.

2.02331 Either a thing has properties which no other has, and then one can distinguish it straight away from the others by a description and refer to it ; or, on the other hand, there are several things which have the totality of their properties in

sam haben, dann ist es überhaupt unmöglich auf eines von ihnen zu zeigen.

Denn, ist das Ding durch nichts hervorgehoben, so kann ich es nicht hervorheben, denn sonst ist es eben hervorgehoben.

2.024 Die Substanz ist das, was unabhängig von dem was der Fall ist, besteht.

2.025 Sie ist Form und Inhalt.

2.0251 Raum, Zeit und Farbe (Färbigkeit) sind Formen der Gegenstände.

2.026 Nur wenn es Gegenstände gibt, kann es eine feste Form der Welt geben.

2.027 Das Feste, das Bestehende und der Gegenstand sind Eins.

2.0271 Der Gegenstand ist das Feste, Bestehende ; die Konfiguration ist das Wechselnde, Unbeständige.

2.0272 Die Konfiguration der Gegenstände bildet den Sachverhalt.

2.03 Im Sachverhalt hängen die Gegenstände ineinander, wie die Glieder einer Kette.

2.031 Im Sachverhalt verhalten sich die Gegenstände in bestimmter Art und Weise zueinander.

2.032 Die Art und Weise, wie die Gegenstände im Sachverhalt zusammenhängen, ist die Struktur des Sachverhaltes.

2.033 Die Form ist die Möglichkeit der Struktur.

2.034 Die Struktur der Tatsache besteht aus den Strukturen der Sachverhalte.

2.04 Die Gesamtheit der bestehenden Sachverhalte ist die Welt.

2.05 Die Gesamtheit der bestehenden Sachverhalte bestimmt auch, welche Sachverhalte nicht bestehen.

2.06 Das Bestehen und Nichtbestehen von Sachverhalten ist die Wirklichkeit.

(Das Bestehen von Sachverhalten nennen wir auch eine positive, das Nichtbestehen eine negative Tatsache.)

2.061 Die Sachverhalte sind von einander unabhängig.

common, and then it is quite impossible to point to any one of them.

For if a thing is not distinguished by anything, I cannot distinguish it—for otherwise it would be distinguished.

2.024　Substance is what exists independently of what is the case.

2.025　It is form and content.

2.0251　Space, time and colour (colouredness) are forms of objects.

2.026　Only if there are objects can there be a fixed form of the world.

2.027　The fixed, the existent and the object are one.

2.0271　The object is the fixed, the existent ; the configuration is the changing, the variable.

2.0272　The configuration of the objects forms the atomic fact.

2.03　In the atomic fact objects hang one in another, like the links of a chain.

2.031　In the atomic fact the objects are combined in a definite way.

2.032　The way in which objects hang together in the atomic fact is the structure of the atomic fact.

2.033　The form is the possibility of the structure.

2.034　The structure of the fact consists of the structures of the atomic facts.

2.04　The totality of existent atomic facts is the world.

2.05　The totality of existent atomic facts also determines which atomic facts do not exist.

2.06　The existence and non-existence of atomic facts is the reality.

(The existence of atomic facts we also call a positive fact, their non-existence a negative fact.)

2.061　Atomic facts are independent of one another.

2.062   Aus dem Bestehen oder Nichtbestehen eines Sachverhaltes kann nicht auf das Bestehen oder Nichtbestehen eines anderen geschlossen werden.

2.063   Die gesamte Wirklichkeit ist die Welt.

2.1   Wir machen uns Bilder der Tatsachen.

2.11   Das Bild stellt die Sachlage im logischen Raume, das Bestehen und Nichtbestehen von Sachverhalten vor.

2.12   Das Bild ist ein Modell der Wirklichkeit.

2.13   Den Gegenständen entsprechen im Bilde die Elemente des Bildes.

2.131   Die Elemente des Bildes vertreten im Bild die Gegenstände.

2.14   Das Bild besteht darin, dass sich seine Elemente in bestimmter Art und Weise zu einander verhalten.

2.141   Das Bild ist eine Tatsache.

2.15   Dass sich die Elemente des Bildes in bestimmter Art und Weise zu einander verhalten stellt vor, dass sich die Sachen so zu einander verhalten.

Dieser Zusammenhang der Elemente des Bildes heisse seine Struktur und ihre Möglichkeit seine Form der Abbildung.

2.151   Die Form der Abbildung ist die Möglichkeit, dass sich die Dinge so zu einander verhalten, wie die Elemente des Bildes.

2.1511   Das Bild ist s o mit der Wirklichkeit verknüpft; es reicht bis zu ihr.

2.1512   Es ist wie ein Masstab an die Wirklichkeit angelegt.

2.15121   Nur die äussersten Punkte der Teilstriche b e r ü h r e n den zu messenden Gegenstand.

2.1513   Nach dieser Auffassung gehört also zum Bilde auch noch die abbildende Beziehung, die es zum Bild macht.

2.1514   Die abbildende Beziehung besteht aus den Zuordnungen der Elemente des Bildes und der Sachen.

2.1515   Diese Zuordnungen sind gleichsam die Fühler

2.062   From the existence or non-existence of an atomic fact we cannot infer the existence or non-existence of another.

2.063   The total reality is the world.

2.1   We make to ourselves pictures of facts.

2.11   The picture presents the facts in logical space, the existence and non-existence of atomic facts.

2.12   The picture is a model of reality.

2.13   To the objects correspond in the picture the elements of the picture.

2.131   The elements of the picture stand, in the picture, for the objects.

2.14   The picture consists in the fact that its elements are combined with one another in a definite way.

2.141   The picture is a fact.

2.15   That the elements of the picture are combined with one another in a definite way, represents that the things are so combined with one another.

This connexion of the elements of the picture is called its structure, and the possibility of this structure is called the form of representation of the picture.

2.151   The form of representation is the possibility that the things are combined with one another as are the elements of the picture.

2.1511   Thus the picture is linked with reality; it reaches up to it.

2.1512   It is like a scale applied to reality.

2.15121   Only the outermost points of the dividing lines *touch* the object to be measured.

2.1513   According to this view the representing relation which makes it a picture, also belongs to the picture.

2.1514   The representing relation consists of the co-ordinations of the elements of the picture and the things.

2.1515   These co-ordinations are as it were the feelers of

der Bildelmente, mit denen das Bild die Wirklichkeit berührt.

2.16 Die Tatsache muss um Bild zu sein, etwas mit dem Abgebildeten gemeinsam haben.

2.161 In Bild und Abgebildetem muss etwas identisch sein, damit das eine überhaupt ein Bild des anderen sein kann.

2.17 Was das Bild mit der Wirklichkeit gemein haben muss, um sie auf seine Art und Weise— richtig oder falsch—abbilden zu können, ist seine Form der Abbildung.

2.171 Das Bild kann jede Wirklichkeit abbilden, deren Form es hat.

Das räumliche Bild alles Räumliche, das farbige alles Farbige, etc.

2.172 Seine Form der Abbildung aber, kann das Bild nicht abbilden ; es weist sie auf.

2.173 Das Bild stellt sein Objekt von ausserhalb dar (sein Standpunkt ist seine Form der Darstellung), darum stellt das Bild sein Objekt richtig oder falsch dar.

2.174 Das Bild kann sich aber nicht ausserhalb seiner Form der Darstellung stellen.

2.18 Was jedes Bild, welcher Form immer, mit der Wirklichkeit gemein haben muss, um sie überhaupt—richtig oder falsch—abbilden zu können, ist die logische Form, das ist, die Form der Wirklichkeit.

2.181 Ist die Form der Abbildung die logische Form, so heisst das Bild das logische Bild.

2.182 Jedes Bild ist a u c h ein logisches. (Dagegen ist z. B. nicht jedes Bild ein räumliches.)

2.19 Das logische Bild kann die Welt abbilden.

2.2 Das Bild hat mit dem Abgebildeten die logische Form der Abbildung gemein.

2.201 Das Bild bildet die Wirklichkeit ab, indem es eine Möglichkeit des Bestehens und Nichtbestehens von Sachverhalten darstellt.

its elements with which the picture touches reality.

2.16 In order to be a picture a fact must have something in common with what it pictures.

2.161 In the picture and the pictured there must be something identical in order that the one can be a picture of the other at all.

2.17 What the picture must have in common with reality in order to be able to represent it after its manner—rightly or falsely—is its form of representation.

2.171 The picture can represent every reality whose form it has.

The spatial picture, everything spatial, the coloured, everything coloured, etc.

2.172 The picture, however, cannot represent its form of representation ; it shows it forth.

2.173 The picture represents its object from without (its standpoint is its form of representation), therefore the picture represents its object rightly or falsely.

2.174 But the picture cannot place itself outside of its form of representation.

2.18 What every picture, of whatever form, must have in common with reality in order to be able to represent it at all—rightly or falsely—is the logical form, that is, the form of reality.

2.181 If the form of representation is the logical form, then the picture is called a logical picture.

2.182 Every picture is *also* a logical picture. (On the other hand, for example, not every picture is spatial.)

2.19 The logical picture can depict the world.

2.2 The picture has the logical form of representation in common with what it pictures.

2.201 The picture depicts reality by representing a possibility of the existence and non-existence of atomic facts.

2.202 Das Bild stellt eine mögliche Sachlage im logischen Raume dar.

2.203 Das Bild enthält die Möglichkeit der Sachlage, die es darstellt.

2.21 Das Bild stimmt mit der Wirklichkeit überein oder nicht; es ist richtig oder unrichtig, wahr oder falsch.

2.22 Das Bild stellt dar, was es darstellt, unabhängig von seiner Wahr- oder Falschheit, durch die Form der Abbildung.

2.221 Was das Bild darstellt, ist sein Sinn.

2.222 In der Übereinstimmung oder Nichtübereinstimmung seines Sinnes mit der Wirklichkeit, besteht seine Wahrheit oder Falschheit.

2.223 Um zu erkennen, ob das Bild wahr oder falsch ist, müssen wir es mit der Wirklichkeit vergleichen.

2.224 Aus dem Bild allein ist nicht zu erkennen, ob es wahr oder falsch ist.

2.225 Ein a priori wahres Bild gibt es nicht.

3 Das logische Bild der Tatsachen ist der Gedanke.

3.001 „Ein Sachverhalt ist denkbar" heisst: Wir können uns ein Bild von ihm machen.

3.01 Die Gesamtheit der wahren Gedanken sind ein Bild der Welt.

3.02 Der Gedanke enthält die Möglichkeit der Sachlage die er denkt. Was denkbar ist, ist auch möglich.

3.03 Wir können nichts Unlogisches denken, weil wir sonst unlogisch denken müssten.

3.031 Man sagte einmal, dass Gott alles schaffen könne, nur nichts, was den logischen Gesetzen zuwider wäre.—Wir könnten nämlich von einer „unlogischen" Welt nicht sagen, wie sie aussähe.

3.032 Etwas „der Logik widersprechendes" in der Sprache darstellen, kann man ebensowenig, wie in der Geometrie eine den Gesetzen des Raumes widersprechende Figur durch ihre Koordinaten

2.202   The picture represents a possible state of affairs in logical space.

2.203   The picture contains the possibility of the state of affairs which it represents.

2.21   The picture agrees with reality or not; it is right or wrong, true or false.

2.22   The picture represents what it represents, independently of its truth or falsehood, through the form of representation.

2.221   What the picture represents is its sense.

2.222   In the agreement or disagreement of its sense with reality, its truth or falsity consists.

2.223   In order to discover whether the picture is true or false we must compare it with reality.

2.224   It cannot be discovered from the picture alone whether it is true or false.

2.225   There is no picture which is a priori true.

3   The logical picture of the facts is the thought.

3.001   "An atomic fact is thinkable"—means: we can imagine it.

3.01   The totality of true thoughts is a picture of the world.

3.02   The thought contains the possibility of the state of affairs which it thinks.
        What is thinkable is also possible.

3.03   We cannot think anything unlogical, for otherwise we should have to think unlogically.

3.031   It used to be said that God could create everything, except what was contrary to the laws of logic. The truth is, we could not *say* of an "unlogical" world how it would look.

3.032   To present in language anything which "contradicts logic" is as impossible as in geometry to present by its co-ordinates a figure which contradicts the laws of space; or to give

darstellen ; oder die Koordinaten eines Punktes angeben, welcher nicht existiert.

3.0321 Wohl können wir einen Sachverhalt räumlich darstellen, welcher den Gesetzen der Physik, aber keinen, der den Gesetzen der Geometrie zuwiderliefe.

3.04 Ein a priori richtiger Gedanke wäre ein solcher, dessen Möglichkeit seine Wahrheit bedingte.

3.05 Nur so könnten wir a priori wissen, dass ein Gedanke wahr ist, wenn aus dem Gedanken selbst (ohne Vergleichsobjekt) seine Wahrheit zu erkennen wäre.

3.1 Im Satz drückt sich der Gedanke sinnlich wahrnehmbar aus.

3.11 Wir benützen das sinnlich wahrnehmbare Zeichen (Laut- oder Schriftzeichen etc.) des Satzes als Projektion der möglichen Sachlage.

Die Projektionsmethode ist das Denken des Satz-Sinnes.

3.12 Das Zeichen, durch welches wir den Gedanken ausdrücken, nenne ich das Satzzeichen. Und der Satz ist das Satzzeichen in seiner projektiven Beziehung zur Welt.

3.13 Zum Satz gehört alles, was zur Projektion gehört ; aber nicht das Projizierte.

Also die Möglichkeit des Projizierten, aber nicht dieses selbst.

Im Satz ist also sein Sinn noch nicht enthalten, wohl aber die Möglichkeit ihn auszudrücken.

(,,Der Inhalt des Satzes'' heisst der Inhalt des sinnvollen Satzes.)

Im Satz ist die Form seines Sinnes enthalten, aber nicht dessen Inhalt.

3.14 Das Satzzeichen besteht darin, dass sich seine Elemente, die Wörter, in ihm auf bestimmte Art und Weise zu einander verhalten.

Das Satzzeichen ist eine Tatsache.

3.141 Der Satz ist kein Wörtergemisch.—(Wie

the co-ordinates of a point which does not exist.

3.0321　We could present spatially an atomic fact which contradicted the laws of physics, but not one which contradicted the laws of geometry.

3.04　An a priori true thought would be one whose possibility guaranteed its truth.

3.05　Only if we could know a priori that a thought is true if its truth was to be recognized from the thought itself (without an object of comparison).

3.1　In the proposition the thought is expressed perceptibly through the senses.

3.11　We use the sensibly perceptible sign (sound or written sign, etc.) of the proposition as a projection of the possible state of affairs.

The method of projection is the thinking of the sense of the proposition.

3.12　The sign through which we express the thought I call the propositional sign. And the proposition is the propositional sign in its projective relation to the world.

3.13　To the proposition belongs everything which belongs to the projection ; but not what is projected.

Therefore the possibility of what is projected but not this itself.

In the proposition, therefore, its sense is not yet contained, but the possibility of expressing it.

("The content of the proposition" means the content of the significant proposition.)

In the proposition the form of its sense is contained, but not its content.

3.14　The propositional sign consists in the fact that its elements, the words, are combined in it in a definite way.

The propositional sign is a fact.

3.141　The proposition is not a mixture of words

das musikalische Thema kein Gemisch von Tönen.)

Der Satz ist artikuliert.

3.142 Nur Tatsachen können einen Sinn ausdrücken, eine Klasse von Namen kann es nicht.

3.143 Dass das Satzzeichen eine Tatsache ist, wird durch die gewöhnliche Ausdrucksform der Schrift oder des Druckes verschleiert.

Denn im gedruckten Satz z. B. sieht das Satzzeichen nicht wesentlich verschieden aus vom Wort.

(So war es möglich, dass Frege den Satz einen zusammengesetzten Namen nannte.)

3.1431 Sehr klar wird das Wesen des Satzzeichens, wenn wir es uns, statt aus Schriftzeichen, aus räumlichen Gegenständen (etwa Tischen, Stühlen, Büchern) zusammengesetzt denken.

Die gegenseitige räumliche Lage dieser Dinge drückt dann den Sinn des Satzes aus.

3.1432 Nicht: ,,Das komplexe Zeichen ,aRb' sagt, dass a in der Beziehung R zu b steht'', sondern: Dass ,,a'' in einer gewissen Beziehung zu ,,b'' steht, sagt, dass aRb.

3.144 Sachlagen kann man beschreiben, nicht benennen.

(Namen gleichen Punkten, Sätze Pfeilen, sie haben Sinn.)

3.2 Im Satze kann der Gedanke so ausgedrückt sein, dass den Gegenständen des Gedankens Elemente des Satzzeichens entsprechen.

3.201 Diese Elemente nenne ich ,,einfache Zeichen'' und den Satz ,,vollständig analysiert''.

3.202 Die im Satze angewandten einfachen Zeichen heissen Namen.

3.203 Der Name bedeutet den Gegenstand. Der Gegenstand ist seine Bedeutung. (,,A'' ist dasselbe Zeichen wie ,,A''.)

3.21 Der Konfiguration der einfachen Zeichen im

(just as the musical theme is not a mixture of tones).

The proposition is articulate.

3.142 Only facts can express a sense, a class of names cannot.

3.143 That the propositional sign is a fact is concealed by the ordinary form of expression, written or printed.

(For in the printed proposition, for example, the sign of a proposition does not appear essentially different from a word. Thus it was possible for Frege to call the proposition a compounded name.)

3.1431 The essential nature of the propositional sign becomes very clear when we imagine it made up of spatial objects (such as tables, chairs, books) instead of written signs.

The mutual spatial position of these things then expresses the sense of the proposition.

3.1432 We must not say, "The complex sign 'aRb' says 'a stands in relation R to b'"; but we must say, "*That* 'a' stands in a certain relation to 'b' says *that aRb*".

3.144 States of affairs can be described but not *named*.

(Names resemble points; propositions resemble arrows, they have sense.)

3.2 In propositions thoughts can be so expressed that to the objects of the thoughts correspond the elements of the propositional sign.

3.201 These elements I call "simple signs" and the proposition "completely analysed".

3.202 The simple signs employed in propositions are called names.

3.203 The name means the object. The object is its meaning. ("A" is the same sign as "A".)

3.21 To the configuration of the simple signs in the

Satzzeichen entspricht die Konfiguration der Gegenstände in der Sachlage.

3.22 Der Name vertritt im Satz den Gegenstand.

3.221 Die Gegenstände kann ich nur nennen. Zeichen vertreten sie. Ich kann nur von ihnen sprechen, sie aussprechen kann ich nicht. Ein Satz kann nur sagen, wie ein Ding ist, nicht was es ist.

3.23 Die Forderung der Möglichkeit der einfachen Zeichen ist die Forderung der Bestimmtheit des Sinnes.

3.24 Der Satz, welcher vom Komplex handelt, steht in interner Beziehung zum Satze, der von dessen Bestandteil handelt.

Der Komplex kann nur durch seine Beschreibung gegeben sein, und diese wird stimmen oder nicht stimmen. Der Satz, in welchem von einem Komplex die Rede ist, wird, wenn dieser nicht existiert, nicht unsinnig, sondern einfach falsch sein.

Dass ein Satzelement einen Komplex bezeichnet, kann man aus einer Unbestimmtheit in den Sätzen sehen, worin es vorkommt. Wir wissen, durch diesen Satz ist noch nicht alles bestimmt. (Die Allgemeinheitsbezeichnung enthält ja ein Urbild.)

Die Zusammenfassung des Symbols eines Komplexes in ein einfaches Symbol kann durch eine Definition ausgedrückt werden.

3.25 Es gibt eine und nur eine vollständige Analyse des Satzes.

3.251 Der Satz drückt auf bestimmte, klar angebbare Weise aus, was er ausdrückt: Der Satz ist artikuliert.

3.26 Der Name ist durch keine Definition weiter zu zergliedern: er ist ein Urzeichen.

3.261 Jedes definierte Zeichen bezeichnet über jene Zeichen, durch welche es definiert wurde; und die Definitionen weisen den Weg.

Zwei Zeichen, ein Urzeichen, und ein durch Urzeichen definiertes, können nicht auf dieselbe

propositional sign corresponds the configuration of the objects in the state of affairs.

3.22   In the proposition the name represents the object.

3.221   Objects I can only *name*. Signs represent them. I can only speak *of* them. I cannot *assert them*. A proposition can only say *how* a thing is, not *what* it is.

3.23   The postulate of the possibility of the simple signs is the postulate of the determinateness of the sense.

3.24   A proposition about a complex stands in internal relation to the proposition about its constituent part.

A complex can only be given by its description, and this will either be right or wrong. The proposition in which there is mention of a complex, if this does not exist, becomes not nonsense but simply false

That a propositional element signifies a complex can be seen from an indeterminateness in the propositions in which it occurs. We *know* that everything is not yet determined by this proposition. (The notation for generality *contains* a prototype.)

The combination of the symbols of a complex in a simple symbol can be expressed by a definition.

3.25   There is one and only one complete analysis of the proposition.

3.251   The proposition expresses what it expresses in a definite and clearly specifiable way : the proposition is articulate.

3.26   The name cannot be analysed further by any definition. It is a primitive sign.

3.261   Every defined sign signifies *via* those signs by which it is defined, and the definitions show the way.

Two signs, one a primitive sign, and one defined by primitive signs, cannot signify in the

49

Art und Weise bezeichnen. Namen k a n n man nicht durch Definitionen auseinanderlegen. (Kein Zeichen, welches allein, selbständig eine Bedeutung hat.)

3.262 Was in den Zeichen nicht zum Ausdruck kommt, das zeigt ihre Anwendung. Was die Zeichen verschlucken, das spricht ihre Anwendung aus.

3.263 Die Bedeutungen von Urzeichen können durch Erläuterungen erklärt werden. Erläuterungen sind Sätze, welche die Urzeichen enthalten. Sie können also nur verstanden werden, wenn die Bedeutungen dieser Zeichen bereits bekannt sind.

3.3 Nur der Satz hat Sinn ; nur im Zusammenhange des Satzes hat ein Name Bedeutung.

3.31 Jeden Teil des Satzes, der seinen Sinn charakterisiert, nenne ich einen Ausdruck (ein Symbol).

(Der Satz selbst ist ein Ausdruck.)

Ausdruck ist alles, für den Sinn des Satzes wesentliche, was Sätze miteinander gemein haben können.

Der Ausdruck kennzeichnet eine Form und einen Inhalt.

3.311 Der Ausdruck setzt die Formen aller Sätze voraus, in welchen er vorkommen kann. Er ist das gemeinsame charakteristische Merkmal einer Klasse von Sätzen.

3.312 Er wird also dargestellt durch die allgemeine Form der Sätze, die er charakterisiert.

Und zwar wird in dieser Form der Ausdruck k o n s t a n t und alles übrige v a r i a b e l sein.

3.313 Der Ausdruck wird also durch eine Variable dargestellt, deren Werte die Sätze sind, die den Ausdruck enthalten.

(Im Grenzfall wird die Variable zur Konstanten, der Ausdruck zum Satz.)

Ich nenne eine solche Variable „Satzvariable".

3.314 Der Ausdruck hat nur im Satz Bedeutung. Jede Variable lässt sich als Satzvariable auffassen.

same way. Names *cannot* be taken to pieces by definition (nor any sign which alone and independently has a meaning).

3.262 What does not get expressed in the sign is shown by its application. What the signs conceal, their application declares.

3.263 The meanings of primitive signs can be explained by elucidations. Elucidations are propositions which contain the primitive signs. They can, therefore, only be understood when the meanings of these signs are already known.

3.3 Only the proposition has sense; only in the context of a proposition has a name meaning.

3.31 Every part of a proposition which characterizes its sense I call an expression (a symbol).

(The proposition itself is an expression.)

Expressions are everything—essential for the sense of the proposition—that propositions can have in common with one another.

An expression characterizes a form and a content.

3.311 An expression presupposes the forms of all propositions in which it can occur. It is the common characteristic mark of a class of propositions.

3.312 It is therefore represented by the general form of the propositions which it characterizes.

And in this form the expression is *constant* and everything else *variable*.

3.313 An expression is thus presented by a variable, whose values are the propositions which contain the expression.

(In the limiting case the variable becomes constant, the expression a proposition.)

I call such a variable a "propositional variable".

3.314 An expression has meaning only in a proposition. Every variable can be conceived as a propositional variable.

(Auch der variable Name.)

3.315 Verwandeln wir einen Bestandteil eines Satzes in eine Variable, so gibt es eine Klasse von Sätzen, welche sämtlich Werte des so entstandenen variablen Satzes sind. Diese Klasse hängt im allgemeinen noch davon ab, was wir, nach willkürlicher Übereinkunft, mit Teilen jenes Satzes meinen. Verwandeln wir aber alle jene Zeichen, deren Bedeutung willkürlich bestimmt wurde, in Variable, so gibt es nun noch immer eine solche Klasse. Diese aber ist nun von keiner Übereinkunft abhängig, sondern nur noch von der Natur des Satzes. Sie entspricht einer logischen Form— einem logischen Urbild.

3.316 Welche Werte die Satzvariable annehmen darf, wird festgesetzt.

Die Festsetzung der Werte i s t die Variable.

3.317 Die Festsetzung der Werte der Satzvariablen ist die A n g a b e d e r S ä t z e, deren gemeinsames Merkmal die Variable ist.

Die Festsetzung ist eine Beschreibung dieser Sätze.

Die Festsetzung wird also nur von Symbolen, nicht von deren Bedeutung handeln.

Und n u r dies ist der Festsetzung wesentlich, d a s s s i e n u r e i n e B e s c h r e i b u n g v o n S y m b o l e n i s t u n d n i c h t s ü b e r d a s B e-z e i c h n e t e a u s s a g t.

Wie die Beschreibung der Sätze geschieht, ist unwesentlich.

3.318 Den Satz fasse ich—wie Frege und Russell— als Funktion der in ihm enthaltenen Ausdrücke auf.

3.32 Das Zeichen ist das sinnlich Wahrnehmbare am Symbol.

3.321 Zwei verschiedene Symbole können also das Zeichen (Schriftzeichen oder Lautzeichen etc.) miteinander gemein haben—sie bezeichnen dann auf verschiedene Art und Weise.

(Including the variable name.)

3.315   If we change a constituent part of a proposition into a variable, there is a class of propositions which are all the values of the resulting variable proposition. This class in general still depends on what, by arbitrary agreement, we mean by parts of that proposition. But if we change all those signs, whose meaning was arbitrarily determined, into variables, there always remains such a class. But this is now no longer dependent on any agreement; it depends only on the nature of the proposition. It corresponds to a logical form, to a logical prototype.

3.316   What values the propositional variable can assume is determined.

The determination of the values *is* the variable.

3.317   The determination of the values of the propositional variable is done by *indicating the propositions* whose common mark the variable is.

The determination is a description of these propositions.

The determination will therefore deal only with symbols not with their meaning.

And *only* this is essential to the determination, *that it is only a description of symbols and asserts nothing about what is symbolized.*

The way in which we describe the propositions is not essential.

3.318   I conceive the proposition—like Frege and Russell—as a function of the expressions contained in it.

3.32   The sign is the part of the symbol perceptible by the senses.

3.321   Two different symbols can therefore have the sign (the written sign or the sound sign) in common—they then signify in different ways.

3.322   Es kann nie das gemeinsame Merkmal zweier Gegenstände anzeigen, dass wir sie mit demselben Zeichen, aber durch zwei verschiedene B e z e i c h - n u n g s w e i s e n bezeichnen. Denn das Zeichen ist ja willkürlich. Man könnte also auch zwei ver- schiedene Zeichen wählen, und wo bliebe dann das Gemeinsame in der Bezeichnung.

3.323   In der Umgangssprache kommt es ungemein häufig vor, dass dasselbe Wort auf verschiedene Art und Weise bezeichnet — also verschiedenen Symbolen angehört —, oder, dass zwei Wörter, die auf verschiedene Art und Weise bezeichnen, äusserlich in der gleichen Weise im Satze ange- wandt werden.

So erscheint das Wort „ist" als Kopula, als Gleichheitszeichen und als Ausdruck der Existenz; „existieren" als intransitives Zeitwort wie „gehen"; „identisch" als Eigenschaftswort; wir reden von E t w a s, aber auch davon, dass e t w a s geschieht.

(Im Satze „Grün ist grün"—wo das erste Wort ein Personenname, das letzte ein Eigenschaftswort ist—haben diese Worte nicht einfach verschiedene Bedeutung, sondern es sind v e r s c h i e d e n e S y m b o l e.)

3.324   So entstehen leicht die fundamentalsten Ver- wechslungen (deren die ganze Philosophie voll ist).

3.325   Um diesen Irrtümern zu entgehen, müssen wir eine Zeichensprache verwenden, welche sie ausschliesst, indem sie nicht das gleiche Zeichen in verschiedenen Symbolen, und Zeichen, welche auf verschiedene Art bezeichnen, nicht äusserlich auf die gleiche Art verwendet. Eine Zeichensprache also, die der l o g i s c h e n Grammatik—der logi- schen Syntax—gehorcht.

(Die Begriffsschrift Frege's und Russell's ist eine solche Sprache, die allerdings noch nicht alle Fehler ausschliesst.)

3.322   It can never indicate the common characteristic of two objects that we symbolize them with the same signs but by different *methods of symbolizing*. For the sign is arbitrary. We could therefore equally well choose two different signs and where then would be what was common in the symbolization.

3.323   In the language of everyday life it very often happens that the same word signifies in two different ways—and therefore belongs to two different symbols — or that two words, which signify in different ways, are apparently applied in the same way in the proposition.

Thus the word "is" appears as the copula, as the sign of equality, and as the expression of existence; "to exist" as an intransitive verb like "to go"; "identical" as an adjective; we speak of *something* but also of the fact of *something* happening.

(In the proposition "Green is green"—where the first word is a proper name and the last an adjective—these words have not merely different meanings but they are *different symbols*.)

3.324   Thus there easily arise the most fundamental confusions (of which the whole of philosophy is full).

3.325   In order to avoid these errors, we must employ a symbolism which excludes them, by not applying the same sign in different symbols and by not applying signs in the same way which signify in different ways. A symbolism, that is to say, which obeys the rules of *logical* grammar—of logical syntax.

(The logical symbolism of Frege and Russell is such a language, which, however, does still not exclude all errors.)

3.326　Um das Symbol am Zeichen zu erkennen, muss man auf den sinnvollen Gebrauch achten.

3.327　Das Zeichen bestimmt erst mit seiner logisch-syntaktischen Verwendung zusammen eine logische Form.

3.328　Wird ein Zeichen n i c h t g e b r a u c h t, so ist es bedeutungslos. Das ist der Sinn der Devise Occams.

(Wenn sich alles so verhält als hätte ein Zeichen Bedeutung, dann hat es auch Bedeutung.)

3.33　In der logischen Syntax darf nie die Bedeutung eines Zeichens eine Rolle spielen ; sie muss sich aufstellen lassen, ohne dass dabei von der B e d e u-t u n g eines Zeichens die Rede wäre, sie darf n u r die Beschreibung der Ausdrücke voraussetzen.

3.331　Von dieser Bemerkung sehen wir in Russell's „Theory of types" hinüber : Der Irrtum Russell's zeigt sich darin, dass er bei der Aufstellung der Zeichenregeln von der Bedeutung der Zeichen reden musste.

3.332　Kein Satz kann etwas über sich selbst aussagen, weil das Satzzeichen nicht in sich selbst enthalten sein kann, (das ist die ganze „Theory of types").

3.333　Eine Funktion kann darum nicht ihr eigenes Argument sein, weil das Funktionszeichen bereits das Urbild seines Arguments enthält und es sich nicht selbst enthalten kann.

Nehmen wir nämlich an, die Funktion F (fx) könnte ihr eigenes Argument sein ; dann gäbe es also einen Satz : „F(F(fx))" und in diesem müssen die äussere Funktion F und die innere Funktion F verschiedene Bedeutungen haben, denn die innere hat die Form $\phi(fx)$, die äussere, die Form $\psi(\phi(fx))$. Gemeinsam ist den beiden Funktionen nur der Buchstabe „F", der aber allein nichts bezeichnet.

Dies wird sofort klar, wenn wir statt „F(F(u))" schreiben „$(\exists\phi): F(\phi u) . \phi u = Fu$".

Hiermit erledigt sich Russell's Paradox.

3.326   In order to recognize the symbol in the sign we must consider the significant use.

3.327   The sign determines a logical form only together with its logical syntactic application.

3.328   If a sign is *not necessary* then it is meaningless. That is the meaning of Occam's razor.

(If everything in the symbolism works as though a sign had meaning, then it has meaning.)

3.33   In logical syntax the meaning of a sign ought never to play a rôle; it must admit of being established without mention being thereby made of the *meaning* of a sign; it ought to presuppose *only* the description of the expressions.

3.331   From this observation we get a further view— into Russell's *Theory of Types*. Russell's error is shown by the fact that in drawing up his symbolic rules he has to speak about the things his signs mean.

3.332   No proposition can say anything about itself, because the propositional sign cannot be contained in itself (that is the "whole theory of types").

3.333   A function cannot be its own argument, because the functional sign already contains the prototype of its own argument and it cannot contain itself.

If, for example, we suppose that the function $F(fx)$ could be its own argument, then there would be a proposition " $F(F(fx))$ ", and in this the outer function F and the inner function F must have different meanings; for the inner has the form $\phi(fx)$, the outer the form $\psi(\phi(fx))$. Common to both functions is only the letter " F ", which by itself signifies nothing.

This is at once clear, if instead of " $F(F(u))$ " we write " $(\exists\phi) : F(\phi u) . \phi u = Fu$ ".

Herewith Russell's paradox vanishes.

3.334   Die Regeln der logischen Syntax müssen sich von selbst verstehen, wenn man nur weiss, wie ein jedes Zeichen bezeichnet.

3.34   Der Satz besitzt wesentliche und zufällige Züge. Zufällig sind die Züge, die von der besonderen Art der Hervorbringung des Satzzeichens herrühren. Wesentlich diejenigen, welche allein den Satz befähigen, seinen Sinn auszudrücken.

3.341   Das Wesentliche am Satz ist also das, was allen Sätzen, welche den gleichen Sinn ausdrücken können, gemeinsam ist.

Und ebenso ist allgemein das Wesentliche am Symbol das, was alle Symbole, die denselben Zweck erfüllen können, gemeinsam haben.

3.3411   Man könnte also sagen : Der eigentliche Name ist das, was alle Symbole, die den Gegenstand bezeichnen, gemeinsam haben.   Es würde sich so successive ergeben, dass keinerlei Zusammensetzung für den Namen wesentlich ist.

3.342   An unseren Notationen ist zwar etwas willkürlich, aber d a s ist nicht willkürlich : Dass, w e n n wir etwas willkürlich bestimmt haben, dann etwas anderes der Fall sein muss.   (Dies hängt von dem W e s e n der Notation ab.)

3.3421   Eine besondere Bezeichnungsweise mag unwichtig sein, aber wichtig ist es immer, dass diese eine m ö g l i c h e Bezeichnungsweise ist.   Und so verhält es sich in der Philosophie überhaupt : Das Einzelne erweist sich immer wieder als unwichtig, aber die Möglichkeit jedes Einzelnen gibt uns einen Aufschluss über das Wesen der Welt.

3.343   Definitionen sind Regeln der Übersetzung von einer Sprache in eine andere. Jede richtige Zeichensprache muss sich in jede andere nach solchen Regeln übersetzen lassen : D i e s ist, was sie alle gemeinsam haben.

3.344   Das, was am Symbol bezeichnet, ist das Gemeinsame aller jener Symbole, durch die das erste den

3.334   The rules of logical syntax must follow of themselves, if we only know how every single sign
signifies.

3.34   A proposition possesses essential and accidental
features.

Accidental are the features which are due to a
particular way of producing the propositional sign.
Essential are those which alone enable the proposition to express its sense.

3.341   The essential in a proposition is therefore that
which is common to all propositions which can
express the same sense.

And in the same way in general the essential in
a symbol is that which all symbols which can
fulfil the same purpose have in common.

3.3411   One could therefore say the real name is that
which all symbols, which signify an object, have
in common.   It would then follow, step by step,
that no sort of composition was essential for a name.

3.342   In our notations there is indeed something
arbitrary, but *this* is not arbitrary, namely that
if we have determined anything arbitrarily, then
something else *must* be the case. (This results
from the *essence* of the notation.)

3.3421   A particular method of symbolizing may be
unimportant, but it is always important that this
is a *possible* method of symbolizing.   And this
happens as a rule in philosophy : The single
thing proves over and over again to be unimportant,
but the possibility of every single thing reveals
something about the nature of the world.

3.343   Definitions are rules for the translation of one
language into another.   Every correct symbolism
must be translatable into every other according
to such rules.   It is *this* which all have in
common.

3.344   What signifies in the symbol is what is
common to all those symbols by which it can

Regeln der logischen Syntax zufolge ersetzt werden kann.

3.3441 Man kann z. B. das Gemeinsame aller Notationen für die Wahrheitsfunktionen so ausdrücken : Es ist ihnen gemeinsam, dass sich alle—z. B.—durch die Notation von „ ~ p" („nicht p") und „p v q"(„p oder q") ersetzen lassen.

(Hiermit ist die Art und Weise gekennzeichnet, wie eine spezielle mögliche Notation uns allgemeine Aufschlüsse geben kann.)

3.3442 Das Zeichen des Komplexes löst sich auch bei der Analyse nicht willkürlich auf, so dass etwa seine Auflösung in jedem Satzgefüge eine andere wäre.

3.4 Der Satz bestimmt einen Ort im logischen Raum. Die Existenz dieses logischen Ortes ist durch die Existenz der Bestandteile allein verbürgt, durch die Existenz des sinnvollen Satzes.

3.41 Das Satzzeichen und die logischen Koordinaten: Das ist der logische Ort.

3.411 Der geometrische und der logische Ort stimmen darin überein, dass beide die Möglichkeit einer Existenz sind.

3.42 Obwohl der Satz nur einen Ort des logischen Raumes bestimmen darf, so muss doch durch ihn schon der ganze logische Raum gegeben sein.

(Sonst würden durch die Verneinung, die logische Summe, das logische Produkt, etc. immer neue Elemente—in Koordination—eingeführt.)

(Das logische Gerüst um das Bild herum bestimmt den logischen Raum. Der Satz durchgreift den ganzen logischen Raum.)

3.5 Das angewandte, gedachte, Satzzeichen ist der Gedanke.

4 Der Gedanke ist der sinnvolle Satz.

4.001 Die Gesamtheit der Sätze ist die Sprache.

4.002 Der Mensch besitzt die Fähigkeit Sprachen zu bauen, womit sich jeder Sinn ausdrücken lässt,

be replaced according to the rules of logical syntax.

3.3441 We can, for example, express what is common to all notations for the truth-functions as follows : It is common to them that they all, for example, *can be replaced* by the notations of " $\sim p$ " (" not p ") and " $p \lor q$ " (" p or q ").

(Herewith is indicated the way in which a special possible notation can give us general information.)

3.3442 The sign of the complex is not arbitrarily resolved in the analysis, in such a way that its resolution would be different in every propositional structure.

3.4 The proposition determines a place in logical space : the existence of this logical place is guaranteed by the existence of the constituent parts alone, by the existence of the significant proposition.

3.41 The propositional sign and the logical co-ordinates : that is the logical place.

3.411 The geometrical and the logical place agree in that each is the possibility of an existence.

3.42 Although a proposition may only determine one place in logical space, the whole logical space must already be given by it.

(Otherwise denial, the logical sum, the logical product, etc., would always introduce new elements —in co-ordination.)

(The logical scaffolding round the picture determines the logical space. The proposition reaches through the whole logical space.)

3.5 The applied, thought, propositional sign is the thought.

4 The thought is the significant proposition.

4.001 The totality of propositions is the language.

4.002 Man possesses the capacity of constructing languages, in which every sense can be expressed,

ohne eine Ahnung davon zu haben, wie und was jedes Wort bedeutet.—Wie man auch spricht, ohne zu wissen, wie die einzelnen Laute hervorgebracht werden.

Die Umgangssprache ist ein Teil des menschlichen Organismus und nicht weniger kompliziert als dieser.

Es ist menschenunmöglich, die Sprachlogik aus ihr unmittelbar zu entnehmen.

Die Sprache verkleidet den Gedanken. Und zwar so, dass man nach der äusseren Form des Kleides, nicht auf die Form des bekleideten Gedankens schliessen kann; weil die äussere Form des Kleides nach ganz anderen Zwecken gebildet ist, als danach, die Form des Körpers erkennen zu lassen.

Die stillschweigenden Abmachungen zum Verständnis der Umgangssprache sind enorm kompliziert.

4.003   Die meisten Sätze und Fragen, welche über philosophische Dinge geschrieben worden sind, sind nicht falsch, sondern unsinnig. Wir können daher Fragen dieser Art überhaupt nicht beantworten, sondern nur ihre Unsinnigkeit feststellen. Die meisten Fragen und Sätze der Philosophen beruhen darauf, das wir unsere Sprachlogik nicht verstehen.

(Sie sind von der Art der Frage, ob das Gute mehr oder weniger identisch sei als das Schöne.)

Und es ist nicht verwunderlich, dass die tiefsten Probleme eigentlich k e i n e Probleme sind.

4.0031   Alle Philosophie ist „Sprachkritik". (Allerdings nicht im Sinne Mauthners.) Russell's Verdienst ist es, gezeigt zu haben, dass die scheinbare logische Form des Satzes nicht seine wirkliche sein muss.

4.01   Der Satz ist ein Bild der Wirklichkeit.

Der Satz ist ein Modell der Wirklichkeit, so wie wir sie uns denken.

4.011   Auf den ersten Blick scheint der Satz—wie er etwa auf dem Papier gedruckt steht—kein Bild der

without having an idea how and what each word means—just as one speaks without knowing how the single sounds are produced.

Colloquial language is a part of the human organism and is not less complicated than it.

From it it is humanly impossible to gather immediately the logic of language.

Language disguises the thought; so that from the external form of the clothes one cannot infer the form of the thought they clothe, because the external form of the clothes is constructed with quite another object than to let the form of the body be recognized.

The silent adjustments to understand colloquial language are enormously complicated.

4.003　　Most propositions and questions, that have been written about philosophical matters, are not false, but senseless.　We cannot, therefore, answer questions of this kind at all, but only state their senselessness. Most questions and propositions of the philosophers result from the fact that we do not understand the logic of our language.

(They are of the same kind as the question whether the Good is more or less identical than the Beautiful.)

And so it is not to be wondered at that the deepest problems are really *no* problems.

4.0031　　All philosophy is "Critique of language" (but not at all in Mauthner's sense).　Russell's merit is to have shown that the apparent logical form of the proposition need not be its real form.

4.01　　The proposition is a picture of reality.

The proposition is a model of the reality as we think it is.

4.011　　At the first glance the proposition—say as it stands printed on paper—does not seem to be a

Wirklichkeit zu sein, von der er handelt. Aber auch die Notenschrift scheint auf den ersten Blick kein Bild der Musik zu sein, und unsere Lautzeichen-(Buchstaben-)Schrift kein Bild unserer Lautsprache.

Und doch erweisen sich diese Zeichensprachen auch im gewöhnlichen Sinne als Bilder dessen, was sie darstellen.

4.012   Offenbar ist, dass wir einen Satz von der Form „aRb" als Bild empfinden. Hier ist das Zeichen offenbar ein Gleichnis des Bezeichneten.

4.013   Und wenn wir in das Wesentliche dieser Bildhaftigkeit eindringen, so sehen wir, dass dieselbe durch s c h e i n b a r e U n r e g e l m ä s s i g k e i t e n (wie die Verwendung der ♯ und ♭ in der Notenschrift) n i c h t gestört wird.

Denn auch diese Unregelmässigkeiten bilden das ab, was sie ausdrücken sollen; nur auf eine andere Art und Weise.

4.014   Die Grammophonplatte, der musikalische Gedanke, die Notenschrift, die Schallwellen, stehen alle in jener abbildenden internen Beziehung zu einander, die zwischen Sprache und Welt besteht.

Ihnen allen ist der logische Bau gemeinsam.

(Wie im Märchen die zwei Jünglinge, ihre zwei Pferde und ihre Lilien. Sie sind alle in gewissem Sinne Eins.)

4.0141   Dass es eine allgemeine Regel gibt, durch die der Musiker aus der Partitur die Symphonie entnehmen kann, durch welche man aus der Linie auf der Grammophonplatte die Symphonie und nach der ersten Regel wieder die Partitur ableiten kann, darin besteht eben die innere Ähnlichkeit dieser scheinbar so ganz verschiedenen Gebilde. Und jene Regel ist das Gesetz der Projektion, welches die Symphonie in die Notensprache projiziert. Sie ist die Regel der Übersetzung der Notensprache in die Sprache der Grammophonplatte.

4.015   Die Möglichkeit aller Gleichnisse, der ganzen

picture of the reality of which it treats. But nor does the musical score appear at first sight to be a picture of a musical piece ; nor does our phonetic spelling (letters) seem to be a picture of our spoken language. And yet these symbolisms prove to be pictures—even in the ordinary sense of the word —of what they represent.

4.012 It is obvious that we perceive a proposition of the form aRb as a picture. Here the sign is obviously a likeness of the signified.

4.013 And if we penetrate to the essence of this pictorial nature we see that this is not disturbed by *apparent irregularities* (like the use of ♯ and ♭ in the score).

For these irregularities also picture what they are to express ; only in another way.

4.014 The gramophone record, the musical thought, the score, the waves of sound, all stand to one another in that pictorial internal relation, which holds between language and the world.

To all of them the logical structure is common.

(Like the two youths, their two horses and their lilies in the story. They are all in a certain sense one.)

4.0141 In the fact that there is a general rule by which the musician is able to read the symphony out of the score, and that there is a rule by which one could reconstruct the symphony from the line on a gramophone record and from this again—by means of the first rule—construct the score, herein lies the internal similarity between these things which at first sight seem to be entirely different. And the rule is the law of projection which projects the symphony into the language of the musical score. It is the rule of translation of this language into the language of the gramophone record.

4.015 The possibility of all similes, of all the

Bildhaftigkeit unserer Ausdrucksweise, ruht in der Logik der Abbildung.

4.016 Um das Wesen des Satzes zu verstehen, denken wir an die Hieroglyphenschrift, welche die Tatsachen die sie beschreibt abbildet.

Und aus ihr wurde die Buchstabenschrift, ohne das Wesentliche der Abbildung zu verlieren.

4.02 Dies sehen wir daraus, dass wir den Sinn des Satzzeichens verstehen, ohne dass er uns erklärt wurde.

4.021 Der Satz ist ein Bild der Wirklichkeit : Denn ich kenne die von ihm dargestellte Sachlage, wenn ich den Satz verstehe. Und den Satz verstehe ich, ohne dass mir sein Sinn erklärt wurde.

4.022 Der Satz z e i g t seinen Sinn.

Der Satz z e i g t, wie es sich verhält, w e n n er wahr ist. Und er s a g t, d a s s es sich so verhält.

4.023 Die Wirklichkeit muss durch den Satz auf ja oder nein fixiert sein.

Dazu muss sie durch ihn vollständig beschrieben werden.

Der Satz ist die Beschreibung eines Sachverhaltes.

Wie die Beschreibung einen Gegenstand nach seinen externen Eigenschaften, so beschreibt der Satz die Wirklichkeit nach ihren internen Eigenschaften.

Der Satz konstruiert eine Welt mit Hilfe eines logischen Gerüstes und darum kann man am Satz auch sehen, wie sich alles Logische verhält, w e n n er wahr ist. Man kann aus einem falschen Satz S c h l ü s s e z i e h e n.

4.024 Einen Satz verstehen, heisst, wissen was der Fall ist, wenn er wahr ist.

(Man kann ihn also verstehen, ohne zu wissen, ob er wahr ist.)

Man versteht ihn, wenn man seine Bestandteile versteht.

4.025 Die Übersetzung einer Sprache in eine andere

imagery of our language, rests on the logic of representation.

4.016   In order to understand the essence of the proposition, consider hieroglyphic writing, which pictures the facts it describes.

And from it came the alphabet without the essence of the representation being lost.

4.02   This we see from the fact that we understand the sense of the propositional sign, without having had it explained to us.

4.021   The proposition is a picture of reality, for I know the state of affairs presented by it, if I understand the proposition. And I understand the proposition, without its sense having been explained to me.

4.022   The proposition *shows* its sense.

The proposition *shows* how things stand, *if* it is true. And it *says*, that they do so stand.

4.023   The proposition determines reality to this extent, that one only needs to say "Yes" or "No" to it to make it agree with reality.

Reality must therefore be completely described by the proposition.

A proposition is the description of a fact.

As the description of an object describes it by its external properties so propositions describe reality by its internal properties.

The proposition constructs a world with the help of a logical scaffolding, and therefore one can actually see in the proposition all the logical features possessed by reality *if* it is true. One can *draw conclusions* from a false proposition.

4.024   To understand a proposition means to know what is the case, if it is true.

(One can therefore understand it without knowing whether it is true or not.)

One understands it if one understands its constituent parts.

4.025   The translation of one language into another

geht nicht so vor sich, dass man jeden S a t z der einen in einen S a t z der anderen übersetzt, sondern nur die Satzbestandteile werden übersetzt.

(Und das Wörterbuch übersetzt nicht nur Substantiva, sondern auch Zeit-, Eigenschafts- und Bindewörter etc. ; und es behandelt sie alle gleich.)

4.026 Die Bedeutungen der einfachen Zeichen (der Wörter) müssen uns erklärt werden, dass wir sie verstehen.

Mit den Sätzen aber verständigen wir uns.

4.027 Es liegt im Wesen des Satzes, dass er uns einen n e u e n Sinn mitteilen kann.

4.03 Ein Satz muss mit alten Ausdrücken einen neuen Sinn mitteilen.

Der Satz teilt uns eine Sachlage mit, also muss er w e s e n t l i c h mit der Sachlage zusammenhängen.

Und der Zusammenhang ist eben, dass er ihr logisches Bild ist.

Der Satz sagt nur insoweit etwas aus, als er ein Bild ist.

4.031 Im Satz wird gleichsam eine Sachlage probeweise zusammengestellt.

Man kann geradezu sagen : statt, dieser Satz hat diesen und diesen Sinn ; dieser Satz stellt diese und diese Sachlage dar.

4.0311 Ein Name steht für ein Ding, ein anderer für ein anderes Ding und untereinander sind sie verbunden, so stellt das Ganze—wie ein lebendes Bild—den Sachverhalt vor.

4.0312 Die Möglichkeit des Satzes beruht auf dem Prinzip der Vertretung von Gegenständen durch Zeichen.

Mein Grundgedanke ist, dass die „logischen Konstanten" nicht vertreten. Dass sich die Logik der Tatsachen nicht vertreten lässt.

4.032 Nur insoweit ist der Satz ein Bild einer Sachlage, als er logisch gegliedert ist.

is not a process of translating each proposition of the one into a proposition of the other, but only the constituent parts of propositions are translated.

(And the dictionary does not only translate substantives but also adverbs and conjunctions, etc., and it treats them all alike.)

4.026　　　The meanings of the simple signs (the words) must be explained to us, if we are to understand them.

By means of propositions we explain ourselves.

4.027　　　It is essential to propositions, that they can communicate a *new* sense to us.

4.03　　　A proposition must communicate a new sense with old words.

The proposition communicates to us a state of affairs, therefore it must be *essentially* connected with the state of affairs.

And the connexion is, in fact, that it is its logical picture.

The proposition only asserts something, in so far as it is a picture.

4.031　　　In the proposition a state of affairs is, as it were, put together for the sake of experiment.

One can say, instead of, This proposition has such and such a sense, This proposition represents such and such a state of affairs.

4.0311　　　One name stands for one thing, and another for another thing, and they are connected together. And so the whole, like a living picture, presents the atomic fact.

4.0312　　　The possibility of propositions is based upon the principle of the representation of objects by signs.

My fundamental thought is that the "logical constants" do not represent. That the *logic* of the facts cannot be represented.

4.032　　　The proposition is a picture of its state of affairs, only in so far as it is logically articulated.

(Auch der Satz „ambulo" ist zusammengesetzt, denn sein Stamm ergibt mit einer anderen Endung und seine Endung mit einem anderen Stamm, einen anderen Sinn.)

4.04 Am Satz muss gerade soviel zu unterscheiden sein, als an der Sachlage die er darstellt.

Die beiden müssen die gleiche logische (mathematische) Mannigfaltigkeit besitzen. (Vergleiche Hertz's Mechanik, über Dynamische Modelle.)

4.041 Diese mathematische Mannigfaltigkeit kann man natürlich nicht selbst wieder abbilden. Aus ihr kann man beim Abbilden nicht heraus.

4.0411 Wollten wir z. B. das, was wir durch „(x) fx" ausdrücken, durch Vorsetzen eines Indexes vor „fx" ausdrücken—etwa so: „Alg. fx", es würde nicht genügen — wir wüssten nicht, was verallgemeinert wurde. Wollten wir es durch einen Index „a" anzeigen—etwa so: „$f(x_a)$" — es würde auch nicht genügen — wir wüssten nicht den Bereich der Allgemeinheitsbezeichnung.

Wollten wir es durch Einführung einer Marke in die Argumentstellen versuchen — etwa so: „(A, A). F (A, A)"—es würde nicht genügen—wir könnten die Identität der Variablen nicht feststellen. U.s.w.

Alle diese Bezeichnungsweisen genügen nicht, weil sie nicht die notwendige mathematische Mannigfaltigkeit haben.

4.0412 Aus demselben Grunde genügt die idealistische Erklärung des Sehens der räumlichen Beziehungen durch die „Raumbrille" nicht, weil sie nicht die Mannigfaltigkeit dieser Beziehungen erklären kann.

4.05 Die Wirklichkeit wird mit dem Satz verglichen.

4.06 Nur dadurch kann der Satz wahr oder falsch sein, indem er ein Bild der Wirklichkeit ist.

4.061 Beachtet man nicht, dass der Satz einen von den Tatsachen unabhängigen Sinn hat, so kann man leicht glauben, dass wahr und falsch gleich-

(Even the proposition "ambulo" is composite, for its stem gives a different sense with another termination, or its termination with another stem.)

4.04   In the proposition there must be exactly as many things distinguishable as there are in the state of affairs, which it represents.

They must both possess the same logical (mathematical) multiplicity (cf. Hertz's Mechanics, on Dynamic Models).

4.041   This mathematical multiplicity naturally cannot in its turn be represented.   One cannot get outside it in the representation.

4.0411   If we tried, for example, to express what is expressed by " $(x) . fx$ " by putting an index before fx, like : "Gen. fx", it would not do, we should not know what was generalized.   If we tried to show it by an index g, like : " $f(r_g)$ " it would not do—we should not know the scope of the generalization.

If we were to try it by introducing a mark in the argument places, like " $(G,G) . F (G,G)$ ", it would not do—we could not determine the identity of the variables, etc.

All these ways of symbolizing are inadequate because they have not the necessary mathematical multiplicity.

4.0412   For the same reason the idealist explanation of the seeing of spatial relations through "spatial spectacles" does not do, because it cannot explain the multiplicity of these relations.

4.05   Reality is compared with the proposition.

4.06   Propositions can be true or false only by being pictures of the reality.

4.061   If one does not observe that propositions have a sense independent of the facts, one can easily believe that true and false are two relations

berechtigte Beziehungen von Zeichen und Bezeichnetem sind.

Man könnte dann z. B. sagen, dass „p" auf die wahre Art bezeichnet, was „ ~ p" auf die falsche Art, etc.

4.062 Kann man sich nicht mit falschen Sätzen, wie bisher mit wahren, verständigen? Solange man nur weiss, dass sie falsch gemeint sind. Nein! Denn, wahr ist ein Satz, wenn es sich so verhält, wie wir es durch ihn sagen; und wenn wir mit „p" ~ p meinen, und es sich so verhält wie wir es meinen, so ist „p" in der neuen Auffassung wahr und nicht falsch.

4.0621 Dass aber die Zeichen „p" und „ ~ p" das gleiche sagen k ö n n e n, ist wichtig. Denn es zeigt, dass dem Zeichen „ ~ " in der Wirklichkeit nichts entspricht.

Dass in einem Satz die Verneinung vorkommt, ist noch kein Merkmal seines Sinnes (~ ~ p = p).

Die Sätze „p" und „ ~ p" haben entgegengesetzten Sinn, aber es entspricht ihnen eine und dieselbe Wirklichkeit.

4.063 Ein Bild zur Erklärung des Wahrheitsbegriffes: Schwarzer Fleck auf weissem Papier; die Form des Fleckes kann man beschreiben, indem man für jeden Punkt der Fläche angibt, ob er weiss oder schwarz ist. Der Tatsache, dass ein Punkt schwarz ist, entspricht eine positive — der, dass ein Punkt weiss (nicht schwarz) ist, eine negative Tatsache. Bezeichne ich einen Punkt der Fläche (einen Frege'schen Wahrheitswert), so entspricht. dies der Annahme, die zur Beurteilung aufgestellt wird, etc. etc.

Um aber sagen zu können, ein Punkt sei schwarz oder weiss, muss ich vorerst wissen, wann man einen Punkt schwarz und wann man ihn weiss nennt; um sagen zu können: „p" ist wahr (oder falsch), muss ich bestimmt

between signs and things signified with equal rights.

One could then, for example, say that "p" signifies in the true way what " $\sim p$ " signifies in the false way, etc.

4.062   Can we not make ourselves understood by means of false propositions as hitherto with true ones, so long as we know that they are meant to be false? No! For a proposition is true, if what we assert by means of it is the case; and if by "p" we mean $\sim p$, and what we mean is the case, then "p" in the new conception is true and not false.

4.0621   That, however, the signs "p" and " $\sim p$ " *can* say the same thing is important, for it shows that the sign " $\sim$ " corresponds to nothing in reality.

That negation occurs in a proposition, is no characteristic of its sense ($\sim \sim p = p$).

The propositions "p" and " $\sim p$ " have opposite senses, but to them corresponds one and the same reality.

4.063   An illustration to explain the concept of truth. A black spot on white paper; the form of the spot can be described by saying of each point of the plane whether it is white or black. To the fact that a point is black corresponds a positive fact; to the fact that a point is white (not black), a negative fact. If I indicate a point of the plane (a truth-value in Frege's terminology), this corresponds to the assumption proposed for judgment, etc. etc.

But to be able to say that a point is black or white, I must first know under what conditions a point is called white or black; in order to be able to say "p" is true (or false) I must have determined under what conditions I call "p" true,

haben, unter welchen Umständen ich „p" wahr nenne, und damit bestimme ich den Sinn des Satzes.

Der Punkt an dem das Gleichnis hinkt ist nun der: Wir können auf einen Punkt des Papiers zeigen, auch ohne zu wissen, was weiss und schwarz ist; einem Satz ohne Sinn aber entspricht gar nichts, denn er bezeichnet kein Ding (Wahrheitswert) dessen Eigenschaften etwa „falsch" oder „wahr" hiessen; das Verbum eines Satzes ist nicht „ist wahr" oder „ist falsch"—wie Frege glaubte—, sondern das, was „wahr ist" muss das Verbum schon enthalten.

4.064 Jeder Satz muss s c h o n einen Sinn haben; die Bejahung kann ihn ihm nicht geben, denn sie bejaht ja gerade den Sinn. Und dasselbe gilt von der Verneinung, etc.

4.0641 Man könnte sagen: Die Verneinung bezieht sich schon auf den logischen Ort, den der verneinte Satz bestimmt.

Der verneinende Satz bestimmt einen a n d e r e n logischen Ort als der verneinte.

Der verneinende Satz bestimmt einen logischen Ort mit Hilfe des logischen Ortes des verneinten Satzes, indem er jenen ausserhalb diesem liegend beschreibt.

Dass man den verneinten Satz wieder verneinen kann, zeigt schon, dass das, was verneint wird, schon ein Satz und nicht erst die Vorbereitung zu einem Satze ist.

4.1 Der Satz stellt das Bestehen und Nichtbestehen der Sachverhalte dar.

4.11 Die Gesamtheit der wahren Sätze ist die gesamte Naturwissenschaft (oder die Gesamtheit der Naturwissenschaften).

4.111 Die Philosophie ist keine der Naturwissenschaften.

(Das Wort „Philosophie" muss etwas bedeuten,

74

and thereby I determine the sense of the proposition.

The point at which the simile breaks down is this: we can indicate a point on the paper, without knowing what white and black are; but to a proposition without a sense corresponds nothing at all, for it signifies no thing (truth-value) whose properties are called "false" or "true"; the verb of the proposition is not "is true" or "is false"—as Frege thought—but that which "is true" must already contain the verb.

4.064   Every proposition must *already* have a sense; assertion cannot give it a sense, for what it asserts is the sense itself.   And the same holds of denial, etc.

4.0641   One could say, the denial is already related to the logical place determined by the proposition that is denied.

The denying proposition determines a logical place *other* than does the proposition denied.

The denying proposition determines a logical place, with the help of the logical place of the proposition denied, by saying that it lies outside the latter place.

That one can deny again the denied proposition, shows that what is denied is already a proposition and not merely the preliminary to a proposition.

4.1   A proposition presents the existence and non-existence of atomic facts.

4.11   The totality of true propositions is the total natural science (or the totality of the natural sciences).

4.111   Philosophy is not one of the natural sciences.

(The word "philosophy" must mean something.

75

was über oder unter, aber nicht neben den Naturwissenschaften steht.)

4.112 Der Zweck der Philosophie ist die logische Klärung der Gedanken.

Die Philosophie ist keine Lehre, sondern eine Tätigkeit.

Ein philosophisches Werk besteht wesentlich aus Erläuterungen.

Das Resultat der Philosophie sind nicht „philosophische Sätze", sondern das Klarwerden von Sätzen.

Die Philosophie soll die Gedanken, die sonst, gleichsam, trübe und verschwommen sind, klar machen und scharf abgrenzen.

4.1121 Die Psychologie ist der Philosophie nicht verwandter als irgend eine andere Naturwissenschaft.

Erkenntnistheorie ist die Philosophie der Psychologie.

Entspricht nicht mein Studium der Zeichensprache dem Studium der Denkprozesse, welches die Philosophen für die Philosophie der Logik für so wesentlich hielten? Nur verwickelten sie sich meistens in unwesentliche psychologische Untersuchungen und eine analoge Gefahr gibt es auch bei meiner Methode.

4.1122 Die Darwinsche Theorie hat mit der Philosophie nicht mehr zu schaffen, als irgend eine andere Hypothese der Naturwissenschaft.

4.113 Die Philosophie begrenzt das bestreitbare Gebiet der Naturwissenschaft.

4.114 Sie soll das Denkbare abgrenzen und damit das Undenkbare.

Sie soll das Undenkbare von innen durch das Denkbare begrenzen.

4.115 Sie wird das Unsagbare bedeuten, indem sie das Sagbare klar darstellt.

4.116 Alles was überhaupt gedacht werden kann,

which stands above or below, but not beside the natural sciences.)

4.112   The object of philosophy is the logical clarification of thoughts.

Philosophy is not a theory but an activity.

A philosophical work consists essentially of elucidations.

The result of philosophy is not a number of " philosophical propositions ", but to make propositions clear.

Philosophy should make clear and delimit sharply the thoughts which otherwise are, as it were, opaque and blurred.

4.1121   Psychology is no nearer related to philosophy, than is any other natural science.

The theory of knowledge is the philosophy of psychology.

Does not my study of sign-language correspond to the study of thought processes which philosophers held to be so essential to the philosophy of logic? Only they got entangled for the most part in unessential psychological investigations, and there is an analogous danger for my method.

4.1122   The Darwinian theory has no more to do with philosophy than has any other hypothesis of natural science.

4.113   Philosophy limits the disputable sphere of natural science.

4.114   It should limit the thinkable and thereby the unthinkable.

It should limit the unthinkable from within through the thinkable.

4.115   It will mean the unspeakable by clearly displaying the speakable.

4.116   Everything that can be thought at all can be

kann klar gedacht werden. Alles was sich aussprechen lässt, lässt sich klar aussprechen.

4.12 Der Satz kann die gesamte Wirklichkeit darstellen, aber er kann nicht das darstellen, was er mit der Wirklichkeit gemein haben muss, um sie darstellen zu können—die logische Form.

Um die logische Form darstellen zu können, müssten wir uns mit dem Satze ausserhalb der Logik aufstellen können, das heisst ausserhalb der Welt.

4.121 Der Satz kann die logische Form nicht darstellen, sie spiegelt sich in ihm.

Was sich in der Sprache spiegelt, kann sie nicht darstellen.

Was s i c h in der Sprache ausdrückt, können w i r nicht durch sie ausdrücken.

Der Satz z e i g t die logische Form der Wirklichkeit.

Er weist sie auf.

4.1211 So zeigt ein Satz „fa", dass in seinem Sinn der Gegenstand a vorkommt, zwei Sätze „fa" und „ga", dass in ihnen beiden von demselben Gegenstand die Rede ist.

Wenn zwei Sätze einander widersprechen, so zeigt dies ihre Struktur ; ebenso, wenn einer aus dem anderen folgt. U.s.w.

4.1212 Was gezeigt werden k a n n, k a n n nicht gesagt werden.

4.1213 Jetzt verstehen wir auch unser Gefühl : dass wir im Besitze einer richtigen logischen Auffassung seien, wenn nur einmal alles in unserer Zeichensprache stimmt.

4.122 Wir können in gewissem Sinne von formalen Eigenschaften der Gegenstände und Sachverhalte bezw. von Eigenschaften der Struktur der Tatsachen reden und in demselben Sinne von formalen Relationen und Relationen von Strukturen.

(Statt Eigenschaft der Struktur sage ich auch

thought clearly.   Everything that can be said can be said clearly.

4.12   Propositions can represent the whole reality, but they cannot represent what they must have in common with reality in order to be able to represent it—the logical form.

To be able to represent the logical form, we should have to be able to put ourselves with the propositions outside logic, that is outside the world.

4.121   Propositions cannot represent the logical form : this mirrors itself in the propositions.

That which mirrors itself in language, language cannot represent.

That which expresses *itself* in language, *we* cannot express by language.

The propositions *show* the logical form of reality.

They exhibit it.

4.1211 Thus a proposition "*fa*" shows that in its sense the object *a* occurs, two propositions "*fa*" and "*ga*" that they are both about the same object.

If two propositions contradict one another, this is shown by their structure ; similarly if one follows from another, etc.

4.1212 What *can* be shown *cannot* be said.

4.1213 Now we understand our feeling that we are in possession of the right logical conception, if only all is right in our symbolism.

4.122   We can speak in a certain sense of formal properties of objects and atomic facts, or of properties of the structure of facts, and in the same sense of formal relations and relations of structures.

(Instead of property of the structure I also say

79

„interne Eigenschaft"; statt Relation der Strukturen „interne Relation".

Ich führe diese Ausdrücke ein, um den Grund der, bei den Philosophen sehr verbreiteten Verwechslung zwischen den internen Relationen und den eigentlichen (externen) Relationen zu zeigen.)

Das Bestehen solcher interner Eigenschaften und Relationen kann aber nicht durch Sätze behauptet werden, sondern es zeigt sich in den Sätzen, welche jene Sachverhalte darstellen und von jenen Gegenständen handeln.

4.1221 Eine interne Eigenschaft einer Tatsache können wir auch einen Zug dieser Tatsache nennen. (In dem Sinn, in welchem wir etwa von Gesichtszügen sprechen.)

4.123 Eine Eigenschaft ist intern, wenn es undenkbar ist, dass ihr Gegenstand sie nicht besitzt.

(Diese blaue Farbe und jene stehen in der internen Relation von heller und dunkler eo ipso. Es ist undenkbar, dass d i e s e beiden Gegenstände nicht in dieser Relation stünden.)

(Hier entspricht dem schwankenden Gebrauch der Worte „Eigenschaft" und „Relation" der schwankende Gebrauch des Wortes „Gegenstand".)

4.124 Das Bestehen einer internen Eigenschaft einer möglichen Sachlage wird nicht durch einen Satz ausgedrückt, sondern es drückt sich in dem sie darstellenden Satz, durch eine interne Eigenschaft dieses Satzes aus.

Es wäre ebenso unsinnig, dem Satze eine formale Eigenschaft zuzusprechen, als sie ihm abzusprechen.

4.1241 Formen kann man nicht dadurch von einander unterscheiden, dass man sagt, die eine habe diese, die andere aber jene Eigenschaft; denn dies setzt voraus, dass es einen Sinn habe, beide Eigenschaften von beiden Formen auszusagen.

4.125 Das Bestehen einer internen Relation zwischen

"internal property"; instead of relation of structures "internal relation".

I introduce these expressions in order to show the reason for the confusion, very widespread among philosophers, between internal relations and proper (external) relations.)

The holding of such internal properties and relations cannot, however, be asserted by propositions, but it shows itself in the propositions, which present the facts and treat of the objects in question.

4.1221   An internal property of a fact we also call a feature of this fact. (In the sense in which we speak of facial features.)

4.123   A property is internal if it is unthinkable that its object does not possess it.

(This blue colour and that stand in the internal relation of brighter and darker eo ipso. It is unthinkable that *these* two objects should not stand in this relation.)

(Here to the shifting use of the words "property" and "relation" there corresponds the shifting use of the word "object".)

4.124   The existence of an internal property of a possible state of affairs is not expressed by a proposition, but it expresses itself in the proposition which presents that state of affairs, by an internal property of this proposition.

It would be as senseless to ascribe a formal property to a proposition as to deny it the formal property.

4.1241   One cannot distinguish forms from one another by saying that one has this property, the other that: for this assumes that there is a sense in asserting either property of either form.

4.125   The existence of an internal relation between

möglichen Sachlagen drückt sich sprachlich durch eine interne Relation zwischen den sie darstellenden Sätzen aus.

4.1251   Hier erledigt sich nun die Streitfrage „ob alle Relationen intern oder extern" seien.

4.1252   Reihen, welche durch i n t e r n e Relationen geordnet sind, nenne ich Formenreihen.

Die Zahlenreihe ist nicht nach einer externen, sondern nach einer internen Relation geordnet.

Ebenso die Reihe der Sätze „aRb",

    „$(\exists x):aRx . xRb$",

    „$(\exists x,y):aRx . xRy . yRb$", u. s. f.

(Steht b in einer dieser Beziehungen zu a, so nenne ich b einen Nachfolger von a.)

4.126   In dem Sinne, in welchem wir von formalen Eigenschaften sprechen, können wir nun auch von formalen Begriffen reden.

(Ich führe diesen Ausdruck ein, um den Grund der Verwechslung der formalen Begriffe mit den eigentlichen Begriffen, welche die ganze alte Logik durchzieht, klar zu machen.)

Dass etwas unter einen formalen Begriff als dessen Gegenstand fällt, kann nicht durch einen Satz ausgedrückt werden. Sondern es zeigt sich an dem Zeichen dieses Gegenstandes selbst. (Der Name zeigt, dass er einen Gegenstand bezeichnet, das Zahlzeichen, dass es eine Zahl bezeichnet etc.)

Die formalen Begriffe können ja nicht, wie die eigentlichen Begriffe, durch eine Funktion dargestellt werden.

Denn ihre Merkmale, die formalen Eigenschaften, werden nicht durch Funktionen ausgedrückt.

Der Ausdruck der formalen Eigenschaft ist ein Zug gewisser Symbole.

Das Zeichen der Merkmale eines formalen Begriffes ist also ein charakteristischer Zug aller Symbole, deren Bedeutungen unter den Begriff fallen.

possible states of affairs expresses itself in language by an internal relation between the propositions presenting them.

4.1251 Now this settles the disputed question "whether all relations are internal or external".

4.1252 Series which are ordered by *internal* relations I call formal series.

The series of numbers is ordered not by an external, but by an internal relation.

Similarly the series of propositions "aRb",

$$\text{"}(\exists x):aRx.xRb\text{"},$$
$$\text{"}(\exists x,y):aRx.xRy.yRb\text{"}, \text{ etc.}$$

(If b stands in one of these relations to a, I call b a successor of a.)

4.126 In the sense in which we speak of formal properties we can now speak also of formal concepts.

(I introduce this expression in order to make clear the confusion of formal concepts with proper concepts which runs through the whole of the old logic.)

That anything falls under a formal concept as an object belonging to it, cannot be expressed by a proposition. But it is shown in the symbol for the object itself. (The name shows that it signifies an object, the numerical sign that it signifies a number, etc.)

Formal concepts cannot, like proper concepts, be presented by a function.

For their characteristics, the formal properties, are not expressed by the functions.

The expression of a formal property is a feature of certain symbols.

The sign that signifies the characteristics of a formal concept is, therefore, a characteristic feature of all symbols, whose meanings fall under the concept.

Der Ausdruck des formalen Begriffes also, eine Satzvariable, in welcher nur dieser charakteristische Zug konstant ist.

4.127 Die Satzvariable bezeichnet den formalen Begriff und ihre Werte die Gegenstände, welche unter diesen Begriff fallen.

4.1271 Jede Variable ist das Zeichen eines formalen Begriffes.

Denn jede Variable stellt eine konstante Form dar, welche alle ihre Werte besitzen, und die als formale Eigenschaft dieser Werte aufgefasst werden kann.

4.1272 So ist der variable Name „x" das eigentliche Zeichen des Scheinbegriffes G e g e n s t a n d.

Wo immer das Wort „Gegenstand" („Ding", „Sache", etc.) richtig gebraucht wird, wird es in der Begriffsschrift durch den variablen Namen ausgedrückt.

Zum Beispiel in dem Satz „es gibt 2 Gegenstände, welche . . ." durch „($\exists$x,y) . . .".

Wo immer es anders, also als eigentliches Begriffswort gebraucht wird, entstehen unsinnige Scheinsätze.

So kann man z. B. nicht sagen „Es gibt Gegenstände", wie man etwa sagt „Es gibt Bücher". Und ebenso wenig „Es gibt 100 Gegenstände", oder „Es gibt $\aleph_0$ Gegenstände".

Und es ist unsinnig, von der A n z a h l a l l e r G e g e n s t ä n d e zu sprechen.

Dasselbe gilt von den Worten ,,Komplex'', ,,Tatsache'', ,,Funktion'', ,,Zahl'', etc.

Sie alle bezeichnen formale Begriffe und werden in der Begriffsschrift durch Variable, nicht durch Funktionen oder Klassen dargestellt. (Wie Frege und Russell glaubten.)

Ausdrücke wie ,,1 ist eine Zahl'', ,,es gibt nur Eine Null" und alle ähnlichen sind unsinnig.

(Es ist ebenso unsinnig zu sagen ,,es gibt nur

The expression of the formal concept is therefore a propositional variable in which only this characteristic feature is constant.

4.127   The propositional variable signifies the formal concept, and its values signify the objects which fall under this concept.

4.1271   Every variable is the sign of a formal concept.

For every variable presents a constant form, which all its values possess, and which can be conceived as a formal property of these values.

4.1272   So the variable name "x" is the proper sign of the pseudo-concept *object*.

Wherever the word "object" ("thing", "entity", etc.) is rightly used, it is expressed in logical symbolism by the variable name.

For example in the proposition "there are two objects which . . .", by "$(\exists x,y) \ldots$".

Wherever it is used otherwise, *i.e.* as a proper concept word, there arise senseless pseudo-propositions.

So one cannot, *e.g.* say "There are objects" as one says "There are books". Nor "There are 100 objects" or "There are $\aleph_0$ objects".

And it is senseless to speak of the *number of all objects*.

The same holds of the words "Complex", "Fact", "Function", "Number", etc.

They all signify formal concepts and are presented in logical symbolism by variables, not by functions or classes (as Frege and Russell thought).

Expressions like "1 is a number", "there is only one number nought", and all like them are senseless.

(It is as senseless to say, "there is only one 1"

eine 1", als es unsinnig wäre, zu sagen : 2 + 2 ist um 3 Uhr gleich 4.)

4.12721 Der formale Begriff ist mit einem Gegenstand, der unter ihn fällt, bereits gegeben. Man kann also nicht Gegenstände eines formalen Begriffes u n d den formalen Begriff selbst als Grundbegriffe einführen. Man kann also z. B. nicht den Begriff der Funktion, und auch spezielle Funktionen (wie Russell) als Grundbegriffe einführen; oder den Begriff der Zahl und bestimmte Zahlen.

4.1273 Wollen wir den allgemeinen Satz : „b ist ein Nachfolger von a" in der Begriffsschrift ausdrücken, so brauchen wir hierzu einen Ausdruck für das allgemeine Glied der Formenreihe : aRb, (ꓱx) : aRx . xRb, (ꓱx,y) : aRx . xRy . yRb, . . . Das allgemeine Glied einer Formenreihe kann man nur durch eine Variable ausdrücken, denn der Begriff : Glied dieser Formenreihe, ist ein f o r m a l e r Begriff. (Dies haben Frege und Russell übersehen; die Art und Weise wie sie allgemeine Sätze, wie den obigen ausdrücken wollen ist daher falsch; sie enthält einen circulus vitiosus.)

Wir können das allgemeine Glied der Formenreihe bestimmen, indem wir ihr erstes Glied angeben und die allgemeine Form der Operation, welche das folgende Glied aus dem vorhergehenden Satz erzeugt.

4.1274 Die Frage nach der Existenz eines formalen Begriffes ist unsinnig. Denn kein Satz kann eine solche Frage beantworten.

(Man kann also z. B. nicht fragen : „Gibt es unanalysierbare Subjekt-Prädikatsätze?")

4.128 Die logischen Formen sind zahllos.

Darum gibt es in der Logik keine ausgezeichneten Zahlen und darum gibt es keinen philosophischen Monismus oder Dualismus, etc.

4.2 Der Sinn des Satzes ist seine Übereinstimmung, und Nichtübereinstimmung mit den Mög-

as it would be to say : $2+2$ is at 3 o'clock equal to 4.)

4.12721   The formal concept is already given with an object, which falls under it. One cannot, therefore, introduce both, the objects which fall under a formal concept *and* the formal concept itself, as primitive ideas. One cannot, therefore, *e.g.* introduce (as Russell does) the concept of function and also special functions as primitive ideas ; or the concept of number and definite numbers.

4.1273   If we want to express in logical symbolism the general proposition "*b* is a successor of *a*" we need for this an expression for the general term of the formal series : aRb, $(\exists x):aRx.xRb$, $(\exists x,y):aRx.xRy.yRb$, . . . The general term of a formal series can only be expressed by a variable, for the concept symbolized by "term of this formal series" is a *formal* concept. (This Frege and Russell overlooked; the way in which they express general propositions like the above is, therefore, false; it contains a vicious circle.)

We can determine the general term of the formal series by giving its first term and the general form of the operation, which generates the following term out of the preceding proposition.

4.1274   The question about the existence of a formal concept is senseless. For no proposition can answer such a question.

(For example, one cannot ask : "Are there unanalysable subject-predicate propositions?")

4.128   The logical forms are *anumerical*.

Therefore there are in logic no pre-eminent numbers, and therefore there is no philosophical monism or dualism, etc.

.4.2   The sense of a proposition is its agreement and disagreement with the possibilities of the

lichkeiten des Bestehens und Nichtbestehens der Sachverhalte.

4.21 Der einfachste Satz, der Elementarsatz, behauptet das Bestehen eines Sachverhaltes.

4.211 Ein Zeichen des Elementarsatzes ist es, dass kein Elementarsatz mit ihm in Widerspruch stehen kann.

4.22 Der Elementarsatz besteht aus Namen. Er ist ein Zusammenhang, eine Verkettung, von Namen.

4.221 Es ist offenbar, dass wir bei der Analyse der Sätze auf Elementarsätze kommen müssen, die aus Namen in unmittelbarer Verbindung bestehen.

Es frägt sich hier, wie kommt der Satzverband zustande.

4.2211 Auch wenn die Welt unendlich komplex ist, so dass jede Tatsache aus unendlich vielen Sachverhalten besteht und jeder Sachverhalt aus unendlich vielen Gegenständen zusammengesetzt ist, auch dann müsste es Gegenstände und Sachverhalte geben.

4.23 Der Name kommt im Satz nur im Zusammenhange des Elementarsatzes vor.

4.24 Die Namen sind die einfachen Symbole, ich deute sie durch einzelne Buchstaben (,,x‘‘, ,,y‘‘, ,,z‘‘) an.

Den Elementarsatz schreibe ich als Funktion der Namen in der Form: ,,fx‘‘, ,,$\phi(x,y,)$‘‘, etc.

Oder ich deute ihn durch die Buchstaben p, q, r an.

4.241 Gebrauche ich zwei Zeichen in ein und derselben Bedeutung, so drücke ich dies aus, indem ich zwischen beide das Zeichen ,, = ‘‘ setze.

,,a = b‘‘ heisst also: das Zeichen ,,a‘‘ ist durch das Zeichen ,,b‘‘ ersetzbar.

(Führe ich durch eine Gleichung ein neues Zeichen ,,b‘‘ ein, indem ich bestimme, es solle ein bereits bekanntes Zeichen ,,a‘‘ ersetzen, so schreibe ich die Gleichung—Definition—(wie Russell) in

existence and non-existence of the atomic facts.

4.21   The simplest proposition, the elementary proposition, asserts the existence of an atomic fact.

4.211   It is a sign of an elementary proposition, that no elementary proposition can contradict it.

4.22   The elementary proposition consists of names. It is a connexion, a concatenation, of names.

4.221   It is obvious that in the analysis of propositions we must come to elementary propositions, which consist of names in immediate combination.

The question arises here, how the propositional connexion comes to be.

4.2211 Even if the world is infinitely complex, so that every fact consists of an infinite number of atomic facts and every atomic fact is composed of an infinite number of objects, even then there must be objects and atomic facts.

4.23   The name occurs in the proposition only in the context of the elementary proposition.

4.24   The names are the simple symbols, I indicate them by single letters (x,y,z).

The elementary proposition I write as function of the names, in the form "fx", "$\phi(x,y)$", etc.

Or I indicate it by the letters p,q,r.

4.241   If I use two signs with one and the same meaning, I express this by putting between them the sign "$=$".

"$a=b$" means then, that the sign "a" is replaceable by the sign "b".

(If I introduce by an equation a new sign "b", by determining that it shall replace a previously known sign "a", I write the equation—definition

der Form „a = b Def.". Die Definition ist eine Zeichenregel.)

4.242 Ausdrücke von der Form „a = b" sind also nur Behelfe der Darstellung; sie sagen nichts über die Bedeutung der Zeichen „a", „b" aus.

4.243 Können wir zwei Namen verstehen, ohne zu wissen, ob sie dasselbe Ding oder zwei verschiedene Dinge bezeichnen?—Können wir einen Satz, worin zwei Namen vorkommen, verstehen, ohne zu wissen, ob sie Dasselbe oder Verschiedenes bedeuten?

Kenne ich etwa die Bedeutung eines englischen und eines gleichbedeutenden deutschen Wortes, so ist es unmöglich, dass ich nicht weiss, dass die beiden gleichbedeutend sind; es ist unmöglich, dass ich sie nicht ineinander übersetzen kann.

Ausdrücke wie „a = a", oder von diesen abgeleitete, sind weder Elementarsätze, noch sonst sinnvolle Zeichen. (Dies wird sich später zeigen.)

4.25 Ist der Elementarsatz wahr, so besteht der Sachverhalt; ist der Elementarsatz falsch, so besteht der Sachverhalt nicht.

4.26 Die Angabe aller wahren Elementarsätze beschreibt die Welt vollständig. Die Welt ist vollständig beschrieben durch die Angaben aller Elementarsätze plus der Angabe, welche von ihnen wahr und welche falsch sind.

4.27 Bezüglich des Bestehens und Nichtbestehens von n Sachverhalten gibt es $K_n = \sum_{\nu=0}^{n} \binom{n}{\nu}$ Möglichkeiten.

Es können alle Kombinationen der Sachverhalte bestehen, die andern nicht bestehen.

4.28 Diesen Kombinationen entsprechen ebenso viele Möglichkeiten der Wahrheit—und Falschheit—von n Elementarsätzen.

4.3 Die Wahrheitsmöglichkeiten der Elementarsätze bedeuten die Möglichkeiten des Bestehens und Nichtbestehens der Sachverhalte.

—(like Russell) in the form "$a = b$ Def.". A definition is a symbolic rule.)

4.242 Expressions of the form "$a = b$" are therefore only expedients in presentation : They assert nothing about the meaning of the signs "a" and "b".

4.243 Can we understand two names without knowing whether they signify the same thing or two different things? Can we understand a proposition in which two names occur, without knowing if they mean the same or different things?

If I know the meaning of an English and a synonymous German word, it is impossible for me not to know that they are synonymous, it is impossible for me not to be able to translate them into one another.

Expressions like "$a = a$", or expressions deduced from these are neither elementary propositions nor otherwise significant signs. (This will be shown later.)

4.25 If the elementary proposition is true, the atomic fact exists ; if it is false the atomic fact does not exist.

4.26 The specification of all true elementary propositions describes the world completely. The world is completely described by the specification of all elementary propositions plus the specification, which of them are true and which false.

4.27 With regard to the existence of n atomic facts there are $K_n = \sum\limits_{\nu=0}^{n} \binom{n}{\nu}$ possibilities.

It is possible for all combinations of atomic facts to exist, and the others not to exist.

4.28 To these combinations correspond the same number of possibilities of the truth—and falsehood —of n elementary propositions.

4.3 The truth-possibilities of the elementary propositions mean the possibilities of the existence and non-existence of the atomic facts.

4.31   Die Wahrheitsmöglichkeiten können wir durch Schemata folgender Art darstellen („W" bedeutet „wahr", „F", „falsch". Die Reihen der „W" und „F" unter der Reihe der Elementarsätze bedeuten in leichtverständlicher Symbolik deren Wahrheitsmöglichkeiten) :

p	q	r		p	q		p
W	W	W		W	W		W
F	W	W		F	W		F
W	F	W		W	F		
W	W	F		F	F		
F	F	W					
F	W	F					
W	F	F					
F	F	F					

4.4   Der Satz ist der Ausdruck der Übereinstimmung und Nichtübereinstimmung mit den Wahrheitsmöglichkeiten der Elementarsätze.

4.41   Die Wahrheitsmöglichkeiten der Elementarsätze sind die Bedingungen der Wahrheit und Falschheit der Sätze.

4.411   Es ist von vornherein wahrscheinlich, dass die Einführung der Elementarsätze für das Verständnis aller anderen Satzarten grundlegend ist. Ja, das Verständnis der allgemeinen Sätze hängt f ü h l b a r von dem der Elementarsätze ab.

4.42   Bezüglich der Übereinstimmung und Nichtübereinstimmung eines Satzes mit den Wahrheitsmöglichkeiten von n Elementarsätzen gibt es

$$\sum_{\kappa=0}^{K_u} \binom{K_n}{\kappa} = L_n \text{ Möglichkeiten.}$$

4.43   Die Übereinstimmung mit den Wahrheitsmö-

4.31   The truth-possibilities can be presented by schemata of the following kind ("T" means "true", "F" "false". The rows of T's and F's under the row of the elementary propositions mean their truth-possibilities in an easily intelligible symbolism).

p	q	r
T	T	T
F	T	T
T	F	T
T	T	F
F	F	T
F	T	F
T	F	F
F	F	F

p	q
T	T
F	T
T	F
F	F

p
T
F

4.4   A proposition is the expression of agreement and disagreement with the truth-possibilities of the elementary propositions.

4.41   The truth-possibilities of the elementary propositions are the conditions of the truth and falsehood of the propositions.

4.411   It seems probable even at first sight that the introduction of the elementary propositions is fundamental for the comprehension of the other kinds of propositions. Indeed the comprehension of the general propositions depends *palpably* on that of the elementary propositions.

4.42   With regard to the agreement and disagreement of a proposition with the truth-possibilities of n elementary propositions there are $\sum_{\kappa=0}^{K_n} \binom{K_n}{\kappa} = L_n$ possibilities.

4.43   Agreement with the truth-possibilities can be

glichkeiten können wir dadurch ausdrücken, indem wir ihnen im Schema etwa das Abzeichen „W" (wahr) zuordnen.

Das Fehlen dieses Abzeichens bedeutet die Nichtübereinstimmung.

4.431　Der Ausdruck der Übereinstimmung und Nichtübereinstimmung mit den Wahrheitsmöglichkeiten der Elementarsätze drückt die Wahrheitsbedingungen des Satzes aus.

Der Satz ist der Ausdruck seiner Wahrheitsbedingungen.

(Frege hat sie daher ganz richtig als Erklärung der Zeichen seiner Begriffsschrift vorausgeschickt. Nur ist die Erklärung des Wahrheitsbegriffes bei Frege falsch: Wären „das Wahre" und „das Falsche" wirklich Gegenstände und die Argumente in $\sim p$ etc. dann wäre nach Frege's Bestimmung der Sinn von „ $\sim p$" keineswegs bestimmt.)

4.44　Das Zeichen, welches durch die Zuordnung jener Abzeichen „W" und der Wahrheitsmöglichkeiten entsteht, ist ein Satzzeichen.

4.441　Es ist klar, dass dem Komplex der Zeichen „F" und „W" kein Gegenstand (oder Komplex von Gegenständen) entspricht; so wenig, wie den horizontalen und vertikalen Strichen oder den Klammern.—„Logische Gegenstände" gibt es nicht.

Analoges gilt natürlich für alle Zeichen, die dasselbe ausdrücken wie die Schemata der „W" und „F".

4.442　Es ist z. B.:

p	q	"
W	W	W
F	W	W
W	F	
„ F	F	W

ein Satzzeichen.

(Frege's „Urteilstrich" „⊢" ist logisch ganz

expressed by co-ordinating with them in the schema the mark " T " (true).

Absence of this mark means disagreement.

4.431　　The expression of the agreement and disagreement with the truth-possibilities of the elementary propositions expresses the truth-conditions of the proposition.

The proposition is the expression of its truth-conditions.

(Frege has therefore quite rightly put them at the beginning, as explaining the signs of his logical symbolism. Only Frege's explanation of the truth-concept is false: if " the true " and " the false " were real objects and the arguments in $\sim p$, etc., then the sense of $\sim p$ would by no means be determined by Frege's determination.)

4.44　　The sign which arises from the co-ordination of that mark " T " with the truth-possibilities is a propositional sign.

4.441　　It is clear that to the complex of the signs " F " and " T " no object (or complex of objects) corresponds; any more than to horizontal and vertical lines or to brackets. There are no " logical objects ".

Something analogous holds of course for all signs, which express the same as the schemata of " T " and " F ".

4.442　　Thus *e.g.*

" p	q	
T	T	T
F	T	T
T	F	
F	F	T "

is a propositional sign.

(Frege's assertion sign " |- " is logically altogether

bedeutungslos; er zeigt bei Frege (und Russell) nur an, dass diese Autoren die so bezeichneten Sätze für wahr halten. „⊢" gehört daher ebenso wenig zum Satzgefüge, wie etwa die Nummer des Satzes. Ein Satz kann unmöglich von sich selbst aussagen, dass er wahr ist.)

Ist die Reihenfolge der Wahrheitsmöglichkeiten im Schema durch eine Kombinationsregel ein für allemal festgesetzt, dann ist die letzte Kolonne allein schon ein Ausdruck der Wahrheitsbedingungen. Schreiben wir diese Kolonne als Reihe hin, so wird das Satzzeichen zu:

„(WW—W) (p , q)" oder deutlicher „(WWFW) (p , q)".

(Die Anzahl der Stellen in der linken Klammer ist durch die Anzahl der Glieder in der rechten bestimmt.)

4.45   Für n Elementarsätze gibt es L_n mögliche Gruppen von Wahrheitsbedingungen.

Die Gruppen von Wahrheitsbedingungen, welche zu den Wahrheitsmöglichkeiten einer Anzahl von Elementarsätzen gehören, lassen sich in eine Reihe ordnen.

4.46   Unter den möglichen Gruppen von Wahrheitsbedingungen gibt es zwei extreme Fälle.

In dem einen Fall ist der Satz für sämtliche Wahrheitsmöglichkeiten der Elementarsätze wahr. Wir sagen, die Wahrheitsbedingungen sind tautologisch.

Im zweiten Fall ist der Satz für sämtliche Wahrheitsmöglichkeiten falsch: Die Wahrheitsbedingungen sind kontradiktorisch.

Im ersten Fall nennen wir den Satz eine Tautologie, im zweiten Fall eine Kontradiktion.

4.461   Der Satz zeigt was er sagt, die Tautologie und die Kontradiktion, dass sie nichts sagen.

Die Tautologie hat keine Wahrheitsbedingungen, denn sie ist bedingungslos wahr; und

meaningless; in Frege (and Russell) it only shows that these authors hold as true the propositions marked in this way.

"⊢" belongs therefore to the propositions no more than does the number of the proposition. A proposition cannot possibly assert of itself that it is true.)

If the sequence of the truth-possibilities in the schema is once for all determined by a rule of combination, then the last column is by itself an expression of the truth-conditions. If we write this column as a row the propositional sign becomes: "$(T\,T\!-\!T)\ (p,q)$", or more plainly: "$(T\,T\,F\,T)\ (p,q)$".

(The number of places in the left-hand bracket is determined by the number of terms in the right-hand bracket.)

4.45   For n elementary propositions there are L_n possible groups of truth-conditions.

The groups of truth-conditions which belong to the truth-possibilities of a number of elementary propositions can be ordered in a series.

4.46   Among the possible groups of truth-conditions there are two extreme cases.

In the one case the proposition is true for all the truth-possibilities of the elementary propositions. We say that the truth-conditions are *tautological*.

In the second case the proposition is false for all the truth-possibilities. The truth-conditions are *self-contradictory*.

In the first case we call the proposition a tautology, in the second case a contradiction.

4.461   The proposition shows what it says, the tautology and the contradiction that they say nothing.

The tautology has no truth-conditions, for it is

die Kontradiktion ist unter keiner Bedingung wahr.

Tautologie und Kontradiktion sind sinnlos.

(Wie der Punkt von dem zwei Pfeile in entgegengesetzter Richtung auseinandergehen.)

(Ich weiss z. B. nichts über das Wetter, wenn ich weiss, dass es regnet oder nicht regnet.)

4.4611 Tautologie und Kontradiktion sind aber nicht unsinnig; sie gehören zum Symbolismus, und zwar ähnlich wie die „0" zum Symbolismus der Arithmetik.

4.462 Tautologie und Kontradiktion sind nicht Bilder der Wirklichkeit. Sie stellen keine mögliche Sachlage dar. Denn jene lässt j e d e mögliche Sachlage zu, diese k e i n e.

In der Tautologie heben die Bedingungen der Übereinstimmung mit der Welt—die darstellenden Beziehungen—einander auf, so dass sie in keiner darstellenden Beziehung zur Wirklichkeit steht.

4.463 Die Wahrheitsbedingungen bestimmen den Spielraum, der den Tatsachen durch den Satz gelassen wird.

(Der Satz, das Bild, das Modell, sind im negativen Sinne wie ein fester Körper, der die Bewegungsfreiheit der anderen beschränkt; im positiven Sinne, wie der von fester Substanz begrenzte Raum, worin ein Körper Platz hat.)

Die Tautologie lässt der Wirklichkeit den ganzen —unendlichen—logischen Raum ; die Kontradiktion erfüllt den ganzen logischen Raum und lässt der Wirklichkeit keinen Punkt. Keine von beiden kann daher die Wirklichkeit irgendwie bestimmen.

4.464 Die Wahrheit der Tautologie ist gewiss, des Satzes möglich, der Kontradiktion unmöglich.

(Gewiss, möglich, unmöglich : Hier haben wir das Anzeichen jener Gradation, die wir in der Wahrscheinlichkeitslehre brauchen.)

4.465 Das logische Produkt einer Tautologie und

unconditionally true ; and the contradiction is on no condition true.

Tautology and contradiction are without sense.

(Like the point from which two arrows go out in opposite directions.)

(I know, *e.g.* nothing about the weather, when I know that it rains or does not rain.)

4.4611   Tautology and contradiction are, however, not nonsensical ; they are part of the symbolism, in the same way that "o" is part of the symbolism of Arithmetic.

4.462   Tautology and contradiction are not pictures of the reality.   They present no possible state of affairs. For the one allows *every* possible state of affairs, the other *none*.

In the tautology the conditions of agreement with the world—the presenting relations—cancel one another, so that it stands in no presenting relation to reality.

4.463   The truth-conditions determine the range, which is left to the facts by the proposition.

(The proposition, the picture, the model, are in a negative sense like a solid body, which restricts the free movement of another : in a positive sense, like the space limited by solid substance, in which a body may be placed.)

Tautology leaves to reality the whole infinite logical space ; contradiction fills the whole logical space and leaves no point to reality. Neither of them, therefore, can in any way determine reality.

4.464   The truth of tautology is certain, of propositions possible, of contradiction impossible.

(Certain, possible, impossible : here we have an indication of that gradation which we need in the theory of probability.)

4.465   The logical product of a tautology and a pro-

eines Satzes sagt dasselbe, wie der Satz. Also ist jenes Produkt identisch mit dem Satz. Denn man kann das Wesentliche des Symbols nicht ändern, ohne seinen Sinn zu ändern.

4.466   Einer bestimmten logischen Verbindung von Zeichen entspricht eine bestimmte logische Verbindung ihrer Bedeutungen; j e d e b e l i e b i g e Verbindung entspricht nur den unverbundenen Zeichen.

Das heisst, Sätze die für jede Sachlage wahr sind, können überhaupt keine Zeichenverbindungen sein, denn sonst könnten ihnen nur bestimmte Verbindungen von Gegenständen entsprechen.

(Und keiner logischen Verbindung entspricht k e i n e Verbindung der Gegenstände.)

Tautologie und Kontradiktion sind die Grenzfälle der Zeichenverbindung, nämlich ihre Auflösung.

4.4661   Freilich sind auch in der Tautologie und Kontradiktion die Zeichen noch mit einander verbunden, d. h. sie stehen in Beziehungen zu einander, aber diese Beziehungen sind bedeutungslos, dem S y m b o l unwesentlich.

4.5   Nun scheint es möglich zu sein, die allgemeinste Satzform anzugeben: das heisst, eine Beschreibung der Sätze i r g e n d e i n e r Zeichensprache zu geben, so dass jeder mögliche Sinn durch ein Symbol, auf welches die Beschreibung passt, ausgedrückt werden kann, und dass jedes Symbol, worauf die Beschreibung passt, einen Sinn ausdrücken kann, wenn die Bedeutungen der Namen entsprechend gewählt werden.

Es ist klar, dass bei der Beschreibung der allgemeinsten Satzform n u r ihr Wesentliches beschrieben werden darf,—sonst wäre sie nämlich nicht die allgemeinste.

Dass es eine allgemeine Satzform gibt, wird dadurch bewiesen, dass es keinen Satz geben darf, dessen Form man nicht hätte voraussehen (d. h.

position says the same as the proposition. Therefore that product is identical with the proposition.
For the essence of the symbol cannot be altered
without altering its sense.

4.466　　To a definite logical combination of signs
corresponds a definite logical combination of their
meanings ; *every arbitrary* combination only corresponds to the unconnected signs.

That is, propositions which are true for every
state of affairs cannot be combinations of signs at
all, for otherwise there could only correspond to
them definite combinations of objects.

(And to no logical combination corresponds *no*
combination of the objects.)

Tautology and contradiction are the limiting
cases of the combinations of symbols, namely their
dissolution.

4.4661　　Of course the signs are also combined with one
another in the tautology and contradiction, *i.e.*
they stand in relations to one another, but these
relations are meaningless, unessential to the
symbol.

4.5　　Now it appears to be possible to give the
most general form of proposition ; *i.e.* to give a
description of the propositions of some one sign
language, so that every possible sense can be
expressed by a symbol, which falls under the
description, and so that every symbol which falls
under the description can express a sense, if
the meanings of the names are chosen accordingly.

It is clear that in the description of the most
general form of proposition *only* what is essential
to it may be described—otherwise it would not be
the most general form.

That there is a general form is proved by the
fact that there cannot be a proposition whose
form could not have been foreseen (*i.e.* constructed).

konstruieren) können.   Die allgemeine Form des Satzes ist: Es verhält sich so und so.

4.51   Angenommen, mir wären alle Elementarsätze gegeben: Dann lässt sich einfach fragen: welche Sätze kann ich aus ihnen bilden. Und das sind alle Sätze und so sind sie begrenzt.

4.52   Die Sätze sind Alles, was aus der Gesamtheit aller Elementarsätze folgt (natürlich auch daraus, dass es die Gesamtheit aller ist). (So könnte man in gewissem Sinne sagen, dass alle Sätze Verallgemeinerungen der Elementarsätze sind.)

4.53   Die allgemeine Satzform ist eine Variable.

5   Der Satz ist eine Wahrheitsfunktion der Elementarsätze.

(Der Elementarsatz ist eine Wahrheitsfunktion seiner selbst.)

5.01   Die Elementarsätze sind die Wahrheitsargumente des Satzes.

5.02   Es liegt nahe, die Argumente von Funktionen mit den Indices von Namen zu verwechseln.   Ich erkenne nämlich sowohl am Argument wie am Index die Bedeutung des sie enthaltenden Zeichens.

In Russell's „+$_c$" ist z. B. „c" ein Index, der darauf hinweist, dass das ganze Zeichen das Additionszeichen für Kardinalzahlen ist.   Aber diese Bezeichnung beruht auf willkürlicher Übereinkunft und man könnte statt „+$_c$" auch ein einfaches Zeichen wählen; in „ ~ p" aber ist „p" kein Index, sondern ein Argument: der Sinn von „ ~ p" kann nicht verstanden werden, ohne dass vorher der Sinn von „p" verstanden worden wäre.   (Im Namen Julius Cäsar ist „Julius" ein Index.   Der Index ist immer ein Teil einer Beschreibung des Gegenstandes, dessen Namen wir ihn anhängen.   Z. B. Der Cäsar aus dem Geschlechte der Julier.)

Die Verwechslung von Argument und Index liegt, wenn ich mich nicht irre, der Theorie Frege's von der Bedeutung der Sätze und Funktionen

The general form of proposition is: Such and such is the case.

4.51 Suppose *all* elementary propositions were given me : then we can simply ask: what propositions I can build out of them. And these are *all* propositions and *so* are they limited.

4.52 The propositions are everything which follows from the totality of all elementary propositions (of course also from the fact that it is the *totality of them all*). (So, in some sense, one could say, that *all* propositions are generalizations of the elementary propositions.)

4.53 The general propositional form is a variable.

5 Propositions are truth-functions of elementary propositions.

(An elementary proposition is a truth-function of itself.)

5.01 The elementary propositions are the truth-arguments of propositions.

5.02 It is natural to confuse the arguments of functions with the indices of names. For I recognize the meaning of the sign containing it from the argument just as much as from the index.

In Russell's " $+_c$ ", for example, " c " is an index which indicates that the whole sign is the addition sign for cardinal numbers. But this way of symbolizing depends on arbitrary agreement, and one could choose a simple sign instead of " $+_c$ ": but in " $\sim p$ " " p " is not an index but an argument ; the sense of " $\sim p$ " *cannot* be understood, unless the sense of " p " has previously been understood. (In the name Julius Cæsar, Julius is an index. The index is always part of a description of the object to whose name we attach it, *e.g.* *The* Cæsar of the Julian gens.)

The confusion of argument and index is, if I am not mistaken, at the root of Frege's theory

zugrunde. Für Frege waren die Sätze der Logik
Namen, und deren Argumente die Indices dieser
Namen.

5.1 Die Wahrheitsfunktionen lassen sich in Reihen
ordnen.

Das ist die Grundlage der Wahrscheinlichkeitslehre.

5.101 Die Wahrheitsfunktionen jeder Anzahl von
Elementarsätzen lassen sich in einem Schema
folgender Art hinschreiben:

(W W W W) (p, q) Tautologie (Wenn p, so p ; und wenn q, so q.) (p ⊃ p . q ⊃ q)
(F W W W) (p, q) in Worten : Nicht beides p und q. (∼ (p . q))
(W F W W) (p, q) „   „   Wenn q, so p. (q ⊃ p)
(W W F W) (p, q) „   „   Wenn p, so q. (p ⊃ q)
(W W W F) (p, q) „   „   p oder q. (pvq)
(F F W W) (p, q) „   „   Nicht q. (∼ q)
(F W F W) (p, q) „   „   Nicht p. (∼ p)
(F W W F) (p, q) „   „   p, oder q, aber nicht beide. (p . ∼ q : v : q . ∼ p)
(W F F W) (p, q) „   „   Wenn p, so q ; und wenn q, so p. (p≡q)
(W F W F) (p, q) „   „   p
(W W F F) (p, q) „   „   q
(F F F W) (p, q) „   „   Weder p noch q. (∼ p . ∼ q) oder (p|q)
(F F W F) (p, q) „   „   p und nicht q. (p . ∼ q)
(F W F F) (p, q) „   „   q und nicht p. (q . ∼ p)
(W F F F) (p, q) „   „   q und p. (q . p)
(F F F F) (p, q) Kontradiktion (p und nicht p ; und q und nicht q.) (p . ∼ p . q . ∼ q)

Diejenigen Wahrheitsmöglichkeiten seiner
Wahrheitsargumente, welche den Satz bewahr-
heiten, will ich seine Wahrheitsgründe
nennen.

5.11 Sind die Wahrheitsgründe, die einer Anzahl
von Sätzen gemeinsam sind, sämtlich auch Wahrheitsgründe eines bestimmten Satzes, so sagen
wir, die Wahrheit dieses Satzes folge aus der
Wahrheit jener Sätze.

5.12 Insbesondere folgt die Wahrheit eines Satzes
,,p'' aus der Wahrheit eines anderen ,,q'', wenn
alle Wahrheitsgründe des zweiten Wahrheitsgründe des ersten sind.

of the meaning of propositions and functions. For Frege the propositions of logic were names and their arguments the indices of these names.

5.1 The truth-functions can be ordered in series.

That is the foundation of the theory of probability.

5.101 The truth-functions of every number of elementary propositions can be written in a schema of the following kind:

(T T T T) (p, q) Tautology (if p then p, and if q then q) $[p \supset p . q \supset q]$
(F T T T) (p, q) in words : Not both p and q. $[\sim (p . q)]$
(T F T T) (p, q) „ „ If q then p. $[q \supset p]$
(T T F T) (p, q) „ „ If p then q. $[p \supset q]$
(T T T F) (p, q) „ „ p or q. $[p \vee q]$
(F F T T) (p, q) „ „ Not q. $[\sim q]$
(F T F T) (p, q) „ „ Not p. $[\sim p]$
(F T T F) (p, q) „ „ p or q, but not both. $[p . \sim q : v : q . \sim p]$
(T F F T) (p, q) „ „ If p, then q; and if q, then p. $[p \equiv q]$
(T F T F) (p, q) „ „ p
(T T F F) (p, q) „ „ q
(F F F T) (p, q) „ „ Neither p nor q. $[\sim p . \sim q$ or $p|q]$
(F F T F) (p, q) „ „ p and not q. $[p . \sim q]$
(F T F F) (p, q) „ „ q and not p. $[q . \sim p]$
(T F F F) (p, q) „ „ p and q. $[p . q]$
(F F F F) (p, q) Contradiction $(p$ and not p; and q and not q.$)[p . \sim p . q . \sim q]$

Those truth-possibilities of its truth-arguments, which verify the proposition, I shall call its *truth-grounds*.

5.11 If the truth-grounds which are common to a number of propositions are all also truth-grounds of some one proposition, we say that the truth of this proposition follows from the truth of those propositions.

5.12 In particular the truth of a proposition p follows from that of a proposition q, if all the truth-grounds of the second are truth-grounds of the first.

5.121   Die Wahrheitsgründe des einen sind in denen des anderen enthalten ; p folgt aus q.

5.122   Folgt p aus q, so ist der Sinn von „p" im Sinne von „q" enthalten.

5.123   Wenn ein Gott eine Welt erschafft, worin gewisse Sätze wahr sind, so schafft er damit auch schon eine Welt, in welcher alle ihre Folgesätze stimmen.   Und ähnlich könnte er keine Welt schaffen, worin der Satz „p" wahr ist, ohne seine sämtlichen Gegenstände zu schaffen.

5.124   Der Satz bejaht jeden Satz der aus ihm folgt.

5.1241   „p . q" ist einer der Sätze, welche „p" bejahen und zugleich einer der Sätze, welche „q" bejahen.

Zwei Sätze sind einander entgegengesetzt, wenn es keinen sinnvollen Satz gibt, der sie beide bejaht.

Jeder Satz der einem anderen widerspricht, verneint ihn.

5.13   Dass die Wahrheit eines Satzes aus der Wahrheit anderer Sätze folgt, ersehen wir aus der Struktur der Sätze.

5.131   Folgt die Wahrheit eines Satzes aus der Wahrheit anderer, so drückt sich dies durch Beziehungen aus, in welchen die Formen jener Sätze zu einander stehen ; und zwar brauchen wir sie nicht erst in jene Beziehungen zu setzen, indem wir sie in einem Satze miteinander verbinden, sondern diese Beziehungen sind intern und bestehen, sobald, und dadurch dass, jene Sätze bestehen.

5.1311   Wenn wir von pvq und ~ p auf q schliessen, so ist hier durch die Bezeichnungsweise die Beziehung der Satzformen von „pvq" und „ ~ p" verhüllt. Schreiben wir aber z. B. statt „pvq" „p|q .|. p|q" und statt „ ~ p" „p|p" (p|q = weder p, noch q), so wird der innere Zusammenhang offenbar.

5.121   The truth-grounds of q are contained in those of p; p follows from q.

5.122   If p follows from q, the sense of "p" is contained in that of "q".

5.123   If a god creates a world in which certain propositions are true, he creates thereby also a world in which all propositions consequent on them are true. And similarly he could not create a world in which the proposition "p" is true without creating all its objects.

5.124   A proposition asserts every proposition which follows from it.

5.1241   "$p.q$" is one of the propositions which assert "p" and at the same time one of the propositions which assert "q".

Two propositions are opposed to one another if there is no significant proposition which asserts them both.

Every proposition which contradicts another, denies it.

5.13   That the truth of one proposition follows from the truth of other propositions, we perceive from the structure of the propositions.

5.131   If the truth of one proposition follows from the truth of others, this expresses itself in relations in which the forms of these propositions stand to one another, and we do not need to put them in these relations first by connecting them with one another in a proposition ; for these relations are internal, and exist as soon as, and by the very fact that, the propositions exist.

5.1311   When we conclude from pvq and $\sim p$ to q the relation between the forms of the propositions "pvq" and "$\sim p$" is here concealed by the method of symbolizing. But if we write, *e.g.* instead of "pvq" "$p|q\ .|.\ p|q$" and instead of "$\sim p$" "$p|p$" ($p|q$ = neither p nor q), then the inner connexion becomes obvious.

(Dass man aus (x). fx auf fa schliessen kann, das zeigt, dass die Allgemeinheit auch im Symbol „(x). fx" vorhanden ist.)

5.132 Folgt p aus q, so kann ich von q auf p schliessen ; p aus q folgern.

Die Art des Schlusses ist allein aus den beiden Sätzen zu entnehmen.

Nur sie selbst können den Schluss rechtfertigen.

„Schlussgesetze", welche—wie bei Frege und Russell—die Schlüsse rechtfertigen sollen, sind sinnlos, und wären überflüssig.

5.133 Alles Folgern geschieht a priori.

5.134 Aus einem Elementarsatz lässt sich kein anderer folgern.

5.135 Auf keine Weise kann aus dem Bestehen irgend einer Sachlage auf das Bestehen einer, von ihr gänzlich verschiedenen Sachlage geschlossen werden.

5.136 Einen Kausalnexus, der einen solchen Schluss rechtfertigte, gibt es nicht.

5.1361 Die Ereignisse der Zukunft k ö n n e n wir nicht aus den gegenwärtigen erschliessen.

Der Glaube an den Kausalnexus ist der A b e r - g l a u b e.

5.1362 Die Willensfreiheit besteht darin, dass zukünftige Handlungen jetzt nicht gewusst werden können. Nur dann könnten wir sie wissen, wenn die Kausalität eine i n n e r e Notwendigkeit wäre, wie die des logischen Schlusses.—Der Zusammenhang von Wissen und Gewusstem, ist der der logischen Notwendigkeit.

(„A weiss, dass p der Fall ist" ist sinnlos, wenn p eine Tautologie ist.)

5.1363 Wenn daraus, dass ein Satz uns einleuchtet, nicht f o l g t, dass er wahr ist, so ist das Einleuchten auch keine Rechtfertigung für unseren Glauben an seine Wahrheit.

5.14 Folgt ein Satz aus einem anderen, so sagt dieser mehr als jener, jener weniger als dieser.

(The fact that we can infer fa from $(x).fx$ shows that generality is present also in the symbol "$(x).fx$".

5.132   If p follows from q, I can conclude from q to p; infer p from q.

The method of inference is to be understood from the two propositions alone.

Only they themselves can justify the inference.

Laws of inference, which — as in Frege and Russell—are to justify the conclusions, are senseless and would be superfluous.

5.133   All inference takes place a priori.

5.134   From an elementary proposition no other can be inferred.

5.135   In no way can an inference be made from the existence of one state of affairs to the existence of another entirely different from it.

5.136   There is no causal nexus which justifies such an inference.

5.1361   The events of the future *cannot* be inferred from those of the present.

Superstition is the belief in the causal nexus.

5.1362   The freedom of the will consists in the fact that future actions cannot be known now. We could only know them if causality were an *inner* necessity, like that of logical deduction.—The connexion of knowledge and what is known is that of logical necessity.

("A knows that p is the case" is senseless if p is a tautology.)

5.1363   If from the fact that a proposition is obvious to us it does not *follow* that it is true, then obviousness is no justification for our belief in its truth.

5.14   If a proposition follows from another, then the latter says more than the former, the former less than the latter.

5.141   Folgt p aus q und q aus p, so sind sie ein und derselbe Satz.

5.142   Die Tautologie folgt aus allen Sätzen : sie sagt Nichts.

5.143   Die Kontradiktion ist das Gemeinsame der Sätze, was kein Satz mit einem anderen gemein hat. Die Tautologie ist das Gemeinsame aller Sätze, welche nichts miteinander gemein haben.

Die Kontradiktion verschwindet sozusagen ausserhalb, die Tautologie innerhalb aller Sätze.

Die Kontradiktion ist die äussere Grenze der Sätze, die Tautologie ihr substanzloser Mittelpunkt.

5.15   Ist W_r die Anzahl der Wahrheitsgründe des Satzes „r", W_{rs} die Anzahl derjenigen Warheitsgründe des Satzes „s", die zugleich Wahrheitsgründe von „r" sind, dann nennen wir das Verhältnis : $W_{rs} : W_r$ das Mass der Wahrscheinlichkeit, welche der Satz „r" dem Satz „s" gibt.

5.151   Sei in einem Schema wie dem obigen in No. 5.101 W_r die Anzahl der „W" im Satze r ; W_{rs} die Anzahl derjenigen „W" im Satze s, die in gleichen Kolonnen mit „W" des Satzes r stehen. Der Satz r gibt dann dem Satze s die Wahrscheinlichkeit : $W_{rs} : W_r$.

5.1511   Es gibt keinen besonderen Gegenstand, der den Wahrscheinlichkeitssätzen eigen wäre.

5.152   Sätze, welche keine Wahrheitsargumente mit einander gemein haben, nennen wir von einander unabhängig.

Zwei Elementarsätze geben einander die Wahrscheinlichkeit $\frac{1}{2}$.

Folgt p aus q, so gibt der Satz „q" dem Satz „p" die Wahrscheinlichkeit 1. Die Gewissheit des logischen Schlusses ist ein Grenzfall der Wahrscheinlichkeit.

(Anwendung auf Tautologie und Kontradiktion.)

5.153   Ein Satz ist an sich weder wahrscheinlich noch

5.141   If p follows from q and q from p then they are one and the same proposition.

5.142   A tautology follows from all propositions: it says nothing.

5.143   Contradiction is something shared by propositions, which *no* proposition has in common with another.   Tautology is that which is shared by all propositions, which have nothing in common with one another.

Contradiction vanishes so to speak outside, tautology inside all propositions.

Contradiction is the external limit of the propositions, tautology their substanceless centre.

5.15   If T_r is the number of the truth-grounds of the proposition "r", T_n the number of those truth-grounds of the proposition "s" which are at the same time truth-grounds of "r", then we call the ratio $T_n : T_r$ the measure of the *probability* which the proposition "r" gives to the proposition "s".

5.151   Suppose in a schema like that above in No. 5.101 T_r is the number of the "T"'s in the proposition r, T_n the number of those "T"'s in the proposition s, which stand in the same columns as "T"'s of the proposition r; then the proposition r gives to the proposition s the probability $T_n : T_r$.

5.1511   There is no special object peculiar to probability propositions.

5.152   Propositions which have no truth-arguments in common with one another we call independent.

Two elementary propositions give to one another the probability $\frac{1}{2}$.

If p follows from q, the proposition q gives to the proposition p the probability 1.   The certainty of logical conclusion is a limiting case of probability.

(Application to tautology and contradiction.)

5.153   A proposition is in itself neither probable nor

unwahrscheinlich. Ein Ereignis trifft ein, oder es trifft nicht ein, ein Mittelding gibt es nicht.

5.154 In einer Urne seien gleichviel weisse und schwarze Kugeln (und keine anderen). Ich ziehe eine Kugel nach der anderen und lege sie wieder in die Urne zurück. Dann kann ich durch den Versuch feststellen, dass sich die Zahlen der gezogenen schwarzen und weissen Kugeln bei fortgesetztem Ziehen einander nähern.

Das ist also kein mathematisches Faktum.

Wenn ich nun sage: Es ist gleich wahrscheinlich, dass ich eine weisse Kugel wie eine schwarze ziehen werde, so heisst das: Alle mir bekannten Umstände (die hypothetisch angenommenen Naturgesetze mitinbegriffen) geben dem Eintreffen des einen Ereignisses nicht mehr Wahrscheinlichkeit als dem Eintreffen des anderen. Das heisst, sie geben—wie aus den obigen Erklärungen leicht zu entnehmen ist—jedem die Wahrscheinlichkeit $\frac{1}{2}$.

Was ich durch den Versuch bestätige ist, dass das Eintreffen der beiden Ereignisse von den Umständen, die ich nicht näher kenne, unabhängig ist.

5.155 Die Einheit des Wahrscheinlichkeitssatzes ist: Die Umstände—die ich sonst nicht weiter kenne—geben dem Eintreffen eines bestimmten Ereignisses den und den Grad der Wahrscheinlichkeit.

5.156 So ist die Wahrscheinlichkeit eine Verallgemeinerung.

Sie involviert eine allgemeine Beschreibung einer Satzform.

Nur in Ermanglung der Gewissheit gebrauchen wir die Wahrscheinlichkeit.—Wenn wir zwar eine Tatsache nicht vollkommen kennen, wohl aber etwas über ihre Form wissen.

(Ein Satz kann zwar ein unvollständiges Bild einer gewissen Sachlage sein, aber er ist immer ein vollständiges Bild.)

improbable. An event occurs or does not occur, there is no middle course.

5.154 In an urn there are equal numbers of white and black balls (and no others). I draw one ball after another and put them back in the urn. Then I can determine by the experiment that the numbers of the black and white balls which are drawn approximate as the drawing continues.

So *this* is not a mathematical fact.

If then, I say, It is equally probable that I should draw a white and a black ball, this means, All the circumstances known to me (including the natural laws hypothetically assumed) give to the occurrence of the one event no more probability than to the occurrence of the other. That is they give — as can easily be understood from the above explanations—to each the probability $\frac{1}{2}$.

What I can verify by the experiment is that the occurrence of the two events is independent of the circumstances with which I have no closer acquaintance.

5.155 The unit of the probability proposition is: The circumstances—with which I am not further acquainted—give to the occurrence of a definite event such and such a degree of probability.

5.156 Probability is a generalization.

It involves a general description of a propositional form. Only in default of certainty do we need probability.

If we are not completely acquainted with a fact, but know *something* about its form.

(A proposition can, indeed, be an incomplete picture of a certain state of affairs, but it is always *a* complete picture.)

Der Wahrscheinlichkeitssatz ist gleichsam ein Auszug aus anderen Sätzen.

5.2 Die Strukturen der Sätze stehen in internen Beziehungen zu einander.

5.21 Wir können diese internen Beziehungen dadurch in unserer Ausdrucksweise hervorheben, dass wir einen Satz als Resultat einer Operation darstellen, die ihn aus anderen Sätzen (den Basen der Operation) hervorbringt.

5.22 Die Operation ist der Ausdruck einer Beziehung zwischen den Strukturen ihres Resultats und ihrer Basen.

5.23 Die Operation ist das, was mit dem einen Satz geschehen muss, um aus ihm den anderen zu machen.

5.231 Und das wird natürlich von ihren formalen Eigenschaften, von der internen Ähnlichkeit ihrer Formen abhängen.

5.232 Die interne Relation, die eine Reihe ordnet, ist äquivalent mit der Operation, durch welche ein Glied aus dem anderen entsteht.

5.233 Die Operation kann erst dort auftreten, wo ein Satz auf logisch bedeutungsvolle Weise aus einem anderen entsteht. Also dort, wo die logische Konstruktion des Satzes anfängt.

5.234 Die Wahrheitsfunktionen der Elementarsätze sind Resultate von Operationen, die die Elementarsätze als Basen haben. (Ich nenne diese Operationen Wahrheitsoperationen.)

5.2341 Der Sinn einer Wahrheitsfunktion von p ist eine Funktion des Sinnes von p.

Verneinung, logische Addition, logische Multiplikation, etc., etc. sind Operationen.

(Die Verneinung verkehrt den Sinn des Satzes.)

5.24 Die Operation zeigt sich in einer Variablen; sie zeigt, wie man von einer Form von Sätzen zu einer anderen gelangen kann.

Sie bringt den Unterschied der Formen zum Ausdruck.

The probability proposition is, as it were, an extract from other propositions.

5.2 The structures of propositions stand to one another in internal relations.

5.21 We can bring out these internal relations in our manner of expression, by presenting a proposition as the result of an operation which produces it from other propositions (the bases of the operation).

5.22 The operation is the expression of a relation between the structures of its result and its bases.

5.23 The operation is that which must happen to a proposition in order to make another out of it.

5.231 And that will naturally depend on their formal properties, on the internal similarity of their forms.

5.232 The internal relation which orders a series is equivalent to the operation by which one term arises from another.

5.233 The first place in which an operation can occur is where a proposition arises from another in a logically significant way ; i.e. where the logical construction of the proposition begins.

5.234 The truth-functions of elementary proposition, are results of operations which have the elementary propositions as bases. (I call these operations, truth-operations.)

5.2341 The sense of a truth-function of p is a function of the sense of p.

Denial, logical addition, logical multiplication, etc. etc., are operations.

(Denial reverses the sense of a proposition.)

5.24 An operation shows itself in a variable ; it shows how we can proceed from one form of proposition to another.

It gives expression to the difference between the forms.

(Und das Gemeinsame zwischen den Basen und dem Resultat der Operation sind eben die Basen.)

5.241 Die Operation kennzeichnet keine Form, sondern nur den Unterschied der Formen.

5.242 Dieselbe Operation, die „q" aus „p" macht, macht aus „q" „r" u. s. f. Dies kann nur darin ausgedrückt sein, dass „p", „q", „r", etc. Variable sind, die gewisse formale Relationen allgemein zum Ausdruck bringen.

5.25 Das Vorkommen der Operation charakterisiert den Sinn des Satzes nicht.

Die Operation sagt ja nichts aus, nur ihr Resultat, und dies hängt von den Basen der Operation ab.

(Operation und Funktion dürfen nicht miteinander verwechselt werden.)

5.251 Eine Funktion kann nicht ihr eigenes Argument sein, wohl aber kann das Resultat einer Operation ihre eigene Basis werden.

5.252 Nur so ist das Fortschreiten von Glied zu Glied in einer Formenreihe (von Type zu Type in den Hierarchien Russells und Whiteheads) möglich. (Russell und Whitehead haben die Möglichkeit dieses Fortschreitens nicht zugegeben, aber immer wieder von ihr Gebrauch gemacht.)

5.2521 Die fortgesetzte Anwendung einer Operation auf ihr eigenes Resultat nenne ich ihre successive Anwendung („O' O' O' a" ist das Resultat der dreimaligen successiven Anwendung von „O' ξ" auf „a").

In einem ähnlichen Sinne rede ich von der successiven Anwendung m e h r e r e r Operationen auf eine Anzahl von Sätzen.

5.2522 Das allgemeine Glied einer Formenreihe a, O' a, O' O' a, ... schreibe ich daher so : „[a, x, O' x]". Dieser Klammerausdruck ist eine Variable. Das erste Glied des Klammerausdruckes ist der An-

(And that which is common to the bases, and the result of an operation, is the bases themselves.)

5.241 The operation does not characterize a form but only the difference between forms.

5.242 The same operation which makes "q" from "p", makes "r" from "q", and so on. This can only be expressed by the fact that "p", "q", "r", etc., are variables which give general expression to certain formal relations.

5.25 The occurrence of an operation does not characterize the sense of a proposition.

For an operation does not assert anything ; only its result does, and this depends on the bases of the operation.

(Operation and function must not be confused with one another.)

5.251 A function cannot be its own argument, but the result of an operation can be its own basis.

5.252 Only in this way is the progress from term to term in a formal series possible (from type to type in the hierarchy of Russell and Whitehead). (Russell and Whitehead have not admitted the possibility of this progress but have made use of it all the same.)

5.2521 The repeated application of an operation to its own result I call its successive application ("$O' \, O' \, O' \, a$" is the result of the threefold successive application of "$O' \, \xi$" to "a").

In a similar sense I speak of the successive application of *several* operations to a number of propositions.

5.2522 The general term of the formal series a, $O' \, a$, $O' \, O' \, a$, ... I write thus : "$[a, x, O' x]$". This expression in brackets is a variable. The first term of the expression is the beginning of the

fang der Formenreihe, das zweite die Form eines beliebigen Gliedes x der Reihe und das dritte die Form desjenigen Gliedes der Reihe, welches auf x unmittelbar folgt.

5.2523 Der Begriff der successiven Anwendung der Operation ist äquivalent mit dem Begriff „und so weiter".

5.253 Eine Operation kann die Wirkung einer anderen rückgängig machen. Operationen können einander aufheben.

5.254 Die Operation kann verschwinden (z. B. die Verneinung in „ ~ ~ p" ~ . ~ p = p).

5.3 Alle Sätze sind Resultate von Wahrheitsoperationen mit den Elementarsätzen.

Die Wahrheitsoperation ist die Art und Weise, wie aus den Elementarsätzen die Wahrheitsfunktion entsteht.

Nach dem Wesen der Wahrheitsoperation wird auf die gleiche Weise, wie aus den Elementarsätzen ihre Wahrheitsfunktion, aus Wahrheitsfunktionen eine Neue. Jede Wahrheitsoperation erzeugt aus Wahrheitsfunktionen von Elementarsätzen wieder eine Wahrheitsfunktion von Elementarsätzen, einen Satz. Das Resultat jeder Wahrheitsoperation mit den Resultaten von Wahrheitsoperationen mit Elementarsätzen ist wieder das Resultat E i n e r Wahrheitsoperation mit Elementarsätzen.

Jeder Satz ist das Resultat von Wahrheitsoperationen mit Elementarsätzen.

5.31 Die Schemata No. 4.31 haben auch dann eine Bedeutung, wenn „p", „q", „r", etc. nicht Elementarsätze sind.

Und es ist leicht zu sehen, dass das Satzzeichen in No. 4.42, auch wenn „p" und „q" Wahrheitsfunktionen von Elementarsätzen sind, Eine Wahrheitsfunktion von Elementarsätzen ausdrückt.

5.32 Alle Wahrheitsfunktionen sind Resultate der

formal series, the second the form of an arbitrary term x of the series, and the third the form of that term of the series which immediately follows x.

5.2523 The concept of the successive application of an operation is equivalent to the concept "and so on".

5.253 One operation can reverse the effect of another. Operations can cancel one another.

5.254 Operations can vanish (*e.g.* denial in "$\sim \sim p$". $\sim \sim p = p$).

5.3 All propositions are results of truth-operations on the elementary propositions.

The truth - operation is the way in which a truth - function arises from elementary propositions.

According to the nature of truth-operations, in the same way as out of elementary propositions arise their truth-functions, from truth-functions arises a new one. Every truth-operation creates from truth-functions of elementary propositions another truth - function of elementary propositions, *i.e.* a proposition. The result of every truth - operation on the results of truth-operations on elementary propositions is also the result of *one* truth - operation on elementary propositions.

Every proposition is the result of truth-operations on elementary propositions.

5.31 The Schemata No. 4.31 are also significant, if "p", "q", "r", etc. are not elementary propositions.

And it is easy to see that the propositional sign in No. 4.42 expresses one truth-function of elementary propositions even when "p" and "q" are truth-functions of elementary propositions.

5.32 All truth-functions are results of the successive

successiven Anwendung einer endlichen Anzahl von Wahrheitsoperationen auf die Elementarsätze.

5.4 Hier zeigt es sich, dass es „logische Gegenstände", „logische Konstante" (im Sinne Freges und Russells) nicht gibt.

5.41 Denn: Alle Resultate von Wahrheitsoperationen mit Wahrheitsfunktionen sind identisch, welche eine und dieselbe Wahrheitsfunktion von Elementarsätzen sind.

5.42 Dass v, ⊃, etc. nicht Beziehungen im Sinne von rechts und links etc. sind, leuchtet ein.

Die Möglichkeit des kreuzweisen Definierens der logischen „Urzeichen" Freges und Russells zeigt schon, dass dies keine Urzeichen sind, und schon erst recht, dass sie keine Relationen bezeichnen.

Und es ist offenbar, dass das „⊃", welches wir durch „ ~ " und „v" definieren, identisch ist mit dem, durch welches wir „v" mit „ ~ " definieren und dass dieses „v" mit dem ersten identisch ist. U. s. w.

5.43 Dass aus einer Tatsache p unendlich viele andere folgen sollten, nämlich ~ ~ p, ~ ~ ~ ~ p, etc., ist doch von vornherein kaum zu glauben. Und nicht weniger merkwürdig ist, dass die unendliche Anzahl der Sätze der Logik (der Mathematik) aus einem halben Dutzend „Grundgesetzen" folgen.

Alle Sätze der Logik sagen aber dasselbe. Nämlich Nichts.

5.44 Die Wahrheitsfunktionen sind keine materiellen Funktionen.

Wenn man z. B. eine Bejahung durch doppelte Verneinung erzeugen kann, ist dann die Verneinung —in irgend einem Sinn—in der Bejahung enthalten? Verneint „ ~ ~ p" ~ p, oder bejaht es p; oder beides?

Der Satz „ ~ ~ p" handelt nicht von der Verneinung wie von einem Gegenstand ; wohl aber ist die Möglichkeit der Verneinung in der Bejahung bereits präjudiziert.

Und gäbe es einen Gegenstand, der „ ~ " hiesse,

application of a finite number of truth-operations to elementary propositions.

5.4　　Here it becomes clear that there are no such things as "logical objects" or "logical constants" (in the sense of Frege and Russell).

5.41　　For all those results of truth-operations on truth-functions are identical, which are one and the same truth-function of elementary propositions.

5.42　　That v, ⊃, etc., are not relations in the sense of right and left, etc., is obvious.

The possibility of crosswise definition of the logical "primitive signs" of Frege and Russell shows by itself that these are not primitive signs and that they signify no relations.

And it is obvious that the "⊃" which we define by means of "∼" and "v" is identical with that by which we define "v" with the help of "∼", and that this "v" is the same as the first, and so on.

5.43　　That from a fact p an infinite number of *others* should follow, namely ∼ ∼ p, ∼ ∼ ∼ ∼ p, etc., is indeed hardly to be believed, and it is no less wonderful that the infinite number of propositions of logic (of mathematics) should follow from half a dozen "primitive propositions".

But all propositions of logic say the same thing. That is, nothing.

5.44　　Truth-functions are not material functions.

If *e.g.* an affirmation can be produced by repeated denial, is the denial—in any sense—contained in the affirmation?

Does "∼ ∼ p" deny ∼ p, or does it affirm p; or both?

The proposition "∼ ∼ p" does not treat of denial as an object, but the possibility of denial is already prejudged in affirmation.

And if there was an object called "∼", then

so müsste „ ~ ~ p" etwas anderes sagen als „p".
Denn der eine Satz würde dann eben von ~
handeln, der andere nicht.

5.441 Dieses Verschwinden der scheinbaren logischen
Konstanten tritt auch ein, wenn „ ~ (ᴕx) . ~ fx"
dasselbe sagt wie „(x) . fx", oder „(ᴕx) . fx . x = a"
dasselbe wie „fa".

5.442 Wenn uns ein Satz gegeben ist, so sind m i t
i h m auch schon die Resultate aller Wahrheitsoperationen, die ihn zur Basis haben, gegeben.

5.45 Gibt es logische Urzeichen, so muss eine richtige
Logik ihre Stellung zueinander klar machen und
ihr Dasein rechtfertigen. Der Bau der Logik a u s
ihren Urzeichen muss klar werden.

5.451 Hat die Logik Grundbegriffe, so müssen sie von
einander unabhängig sein. Ist ein Grundbegriff
eingeführt, so muss er in allen Verbindungen
eingeführt sein, worin er überhaupt vorkommt. Man
kann ihn also nicht zuerst für e i n e Verbindung,
dann noch einmal für eine andere einführen.
Z. B.: Ist die Verneinung eingeführt, so müssen
wir sie jetzt in Sätzen von der Form „ ~ p" ebenso
verstehen, wie in Sätzen wie „ ~ (pvq)", „(ᴕx) . ~ fx"
u. a. Wir dürfen sie nicht erst für die eine Klasse
von Fällen, dann für die andere einführen, denn es
bliebe dann zweifelhaft, ob ihre Bedeutung in beiden
Fällen die gleiche wäre und es wäre kein Grund
vorhanden, in beiden Fällen dieselbe Art der
Zeichenverbindung zu benützen.

(Kurz, für die Einführung der Urzeichen gilt,
mutatis mutandis, dasselbe, was Frege („Grundgesetze der Arithmetik") für die Einführung von
Zeichen durch Definitionen gesagt hat.)

5.452 Die Einführung eines neuen Behelfes in den Symbolismus der Logik muss immer ein folgenschweres
Ereignis sein. Kein neuer Behelf darf in die Logik—
sozusagen, mit ganz unschuldiger Miene—in Klammern oder unter dem Striche eingeführt werden.

" $\sim \sim p$ " would have to say something other than " p ". For the one proposition would then treat of $\sim$, the other would not.

5.441   This disappearance of the apparent logical constants also occurs if " $\sim (\exists x) . \sim fx$ " says the same as " $(x) . fx$ ", or " $(\exists x) . fx . x = a$ " the same as " fa ".

5.442   If a proposition is given to us then the results of all truth-operations which have it as their basis are given *with* it.

5.45   If there are logical primitive signs a correct logic must make clear their position relative to one another and justify their existence. The construction of logic *out of* its primitive signs must become clear.

5.451   If logic has primitive ideas these must be independent of one another. If a primitive idea is introduced it must be introduced in all contexts in which it occurs at all. One cannot therefore introduce it for *one* context and then again for another. For example, if denial is introduced, we must understand it in propositions of the form " $\sim p$ ", just as in propositions like " $\sim (p \vee q)$ ", " $(\exists x) . \sim fx$ " and others. We may not first introduce it for one class of cases and then for another, for it would then remain doubtful whether its meaning in the two cases was the same, and there would be no reason to use the same way of symbolizing in the two cases.

(In short, what Frege ("Grundgesetze der Arithmetik") has said about the introduction of signs by definitions holds, mutatis mutandis, for the introduction of primitive signs also.)

5.452   The introduction of a new expedient in the symbolism of logic must always be an event full of consequences. No new symbol may be introduced in logic in brackets or in the margin—with, so to speak, an entirely innocent face.

(So kommen in den „Principia Mathematica" von Russell und Whitehead Definitionen und Grundgesetze in Worten vor. Warum hier plötzlich Worte? Dies bedürfte einer Rechtfertigung. Sie fehlt und muss fehlen, da das Vorgehen tatsächlich unerlaubt ist.)

Hat sich aber die Einführung eines neuen Behelfes an einer Stelle als nötig erwiesen, so muss man sich nun sofort fragen: Wo muss dieser Behelf nun immer angewandt werden? Seine Stellung in der Logik muss nun erklärt werden.

5.453 Alle Zahlen der Logik müssen sich rechtfertigen lassen.

Oder vielmehr: Es muss sich herausstellen, dass es in der Logik keine Zahlen gibt.

Es gibt keine ausgezeichneten Zahlen.

5.454 In der Logik gibt es kein Nebeneinander, kann es keine Klassifikation geben.

In der Logik kann es nicht Allgemeineres und Spezielleres geben.

5.4541 Die Lösungen der logischen Probleme müssen einfach sein, denn sie setzen den Standard der Einfachheit.

Die Menschen haben immer geahnt, dass es ein Gebiet von Fragen geben müsse, deren Antworten —a priori—symmetrisch, und zu einem abgeschlossenen, regelmässigen Gebilde vereint liegen.

Ein Gebiet, in dem der Satz gilt: simplex sigillum veri.

5.46 Wenn man die logischen Zeichen richtig einführte, so hätte man damit auch schon den Sinn aller ihrer Kombinationen eingeführt; also nicht nur „pvq" sondern auch schon „ ~ (p v ~ q)" etc. etc. Man hätte damit auch schon die Wirkung aller nur möglichen Kombinationen von Klammern eingeführt. Und damit wäre es klar geworden, dass die eigentlichen allgemeinen Urzeichen nicht

(Thus in the "Principia Mathematica" of Russell and Whitehead there occur definitions and primitive propositions in words. Why suddenly words here? This would need a justification. There was none, and can be none for the process is actually not allowed.)

But if the introduction of a new expedient has proved necessary in one place, we must immediately ask: Where is this expedient *always* to be used? Its position in logic must be made clear.

5.453 All numbers in logic must be capable of justification.

Or rather it must become plain that there are no numbers in logic.

There are no pre-eminent numbers.

5.454 In logic there is no side by side, there can be no classification.

In logic there cannot be a more general and a more special.

5.4541 The solution of logical problems must be neat for they set the standard of neatness.

Men have always thought that there must be a sphere of questions whose answers — a priori — are symmetrical and united into a closed regular structure.

A sphere in which the proposition, simplex sigillum veri, is valid.

5.46 When we have rightly introduced the logical signs, the sense of all their combinations has been already introduced with them : therefore not only "$p v q$" but also "$\sim (p v \sim q)$", etc. etc. We should then already have introduced the effect of all possible combinations of brackets; and it would then have become clear that the proper general primitive signs are not "$p v q$", "$(\exists x).fx$", etc.,

die „pvq", „(ᴈx). fx", etc. sind, sondern die allgemeinste Form ihrer Kombinationen.

5.461 Bedeutungsvoll ist die scheinbar unwichtige
Tatsache, dass die logischen Scheinbeziehungen,
wie v und ⊃, der Klammern bedürfen—im Gegensatz zu den wirklichen Beziehungen.

Die Benützung der Klammern mit jenen scheinbaren Urzeichen deutet ja schon darauf hin, dass
diese nicht die wirklichen Urzeichen sind. Und
es wird doch wohl niemand glauben, dass die
Klammern eine selbständige Bedeutung haben.

5.4611 Die logischen Operationszeichen sind Inter-
punktionen.

5.47 Es ist klar, dass alles was sich überhaupt v o n
v o r n h e r e i n über die Form aller Sätze sagen
lässt, sich a u f e i n m a l sagen lassen muss.

Sind ja schon im Elementarsatze alle logischen
Operationen enthalten. Denn „fa" sagt dasselbe
wie „(ᴈx). fx . x=a".

Wo Zusammengesetztheit ist, da ist Argument
und Funktion, und wo diese sind, sind bereits alle
logischen Konstanten.

Man könnte sagen : Die Eine logische Konstante
ist das, was a l l e Sätze, ihrer Natur nach, mit
einander gemein haben.

Das aber ist die allgemeine Satzform.

5.471 Die allgemeine Satzform ist das Wesen des
Satzes.

5.4711 Das Wesen des Satzes angeben, heisst, das
Wesen aller Beschreibung angeben, also das
Wesen der Welt.

5.472 Die Beschreibung der allgemeinsten Satzform
ist die Beschreibung des einen und einzigen
allgemeinen Urzeichens der Logik.

5.473 Die Logik muss für sich selber sorgen.

Ein mögliches Zeichen muss auch bezeichnen
können. Alles was in der Logik möglich ist, ist
auch erlaubt. („Sokrates ist identisch" heisst darum

but the most general form of their combinations.

5.461   The apparently unimportant fact that the apparent relations like v and ⊃ need brackets—unlike real relations—is of great importance.

The use of brackets with these apparent primitive signs shows that these are not the real primitive signs; and nobody of course would believe that the brackets have meaning by themselves.

5.4611   Logical operation signs are punctuations.

5.47   It is clear that everything which can be said *beforehand* about the form of *all* propositions at all can be said *on one occasion*.

For all logical operations are already contained in the elementary proposition. For "*fa*" says the same as "$(\exists x) . fx . x = a$".

Where there is composition, there is argument and function, and where these are, all logical constants already are.

One could say : the one logical constant is that which *all* propositions, according to their nature, have in common with one another.

That however is the general form of proposition.

5.471   The general form of proposition is the essence of proposition.

5.4711   To give the essence of proposition means to give the essence of all description, therefore the essence of the world.

5.472   The description of the most general propositional form is the description of the one and only general primitive sign in logic.

5.473   Logic must take care of itself.

A *possible* sign must also be able to signify. Everything which is possible in logic is also permitted. ("Socrates is identical" means nothing

nichts, weil es keine Eigenschaft gibt, die „identisch" heisst. Der Satz ist unsinnig, weil wir eine willkürliche Bestimmung nicht getroffen haben, aber nicht darum, weil das Symbol an und für sich unerlaubt wäre.) Wir können uns, in gewissem Sinne, nicht in der Logik irren.

5.4731 Das Einleuchten, von dem Russell so viel sprach, kann nur dadurch in der Logik entbehrlich werden, dass die Sprache selbst jeden logischen Fehler verhindert.—Dass die Logik a priori ist, besteht darin, dass nicht unlogisch gedacht werden kann.

5.4732 Wir können einem Zeichen nicht den unrechten Sinn geben.

5.47321 Occams Devise ist natürlich keine willkürliche, oder durch ihren praktischen Erfolg gerechtfertigte, Regel: Sie besagt, dass unnötige Zeicheneinheiten nichts bedeuten.

Zeichen, die Einen Zweck erfüllen, sind logisch äquivalent, Zeichen, die keinen Zweck erfüllen, logisch bedeutungslos.

5.4733 Frege sagt: Jeder rechtmässig gebildete Satz muss einen Sinn haben; und ich sage: Jeder mögliche Satz ist rechtmässig gebildet, und wenn er keinen Sinn hat, so kann das nur daran liegen, dass wir einigen seiner Bestandteile keine Bedeutung gegeben haben.

(Wenn wir auch glauben, es getan zu haben.)

So sagt „Sokrates ist identisch" darum nichts, weil wir dem Wort „identisch" als Eigenschaftswort keine Bedeutung gegeben haben. Denn, wenn es als Gleichheitszeichen auftritt, so symbolisiert es auf ganz andere Art und Weise — die bezeichnende Beziehung ist eine andere, — also ist auch das Symbol in beiden Fällen ganz verschieden; die beiden Symbole haben nur das Zeichen zufällig miteinander gemein.

because there is no property which is called "identical". The proposition is senseless because we have not made some arbitrary determination, not because the symbol is in itself unpermissible.)

In a certain sense we cannot make mistakes in logic.

5.4731   Self-evidence, of which Russell has said so much, can only be discarded in logic by language itself preventing every logical mistake. That logic is a priori consists in the fact that we *cannot* think illogically.

5.4732   We cannot give a sign the wrong sense.

5.47321   Occam's razor is, of course, not an arbitrary rule nor one justified by its practical success. It simply says that *unnecessary* elements in a symbolism mean nothing.

Signs which serve *one* purpose are logically equivalent, signs which serve *no* purpose are logically meaningless.

5.4733   Frege says : Every legitimately constructed proposition must have a sense ; and I say : Every possible proposition is legitimately constructed, and if it has no sense this can only be because we have given no *meaning* to some of its constituent parts.

(Even if we believe that we have done so.)

Thus "Socrates is identical" says nothing, because we have given *no* meaning to the word "identical" as *adjective*. For when it occurs as the sign of equality it symbolizes in an entirely different way—the symbolizing relation is another —therefore the symbol is in the two cases entirely different ; the two symbols have the sign in common with one another only by accident.

5.474   Die Anzahl der nötigen Grundoperationen hängt nur von unserer Notation ab.

5.475   Es kommt nur darauf an, ein Zeichensystem von einer bestimmten Anzahl von Dimensionen — von einer bestimmten mathematischen Mannigfaltigkeit —zu bilden.

5.476   Es ist klar, dass es sich hier nicht um eine Anzahl von Grundbegriffen handelt, die bezeichnet werden müssen, sondern um den Ausdruck einer Regel.

5.5   Jede Wahrheitsfunktion ist ein Resultat der successiven Anwendung der Operation (-----W) $(\xi, \ldots)$ auf Elementarsätze.

Diese Operation verneint sämtliche Sätze in der rechten Klammer und ich nenne sie die Negation dieser Sätze.

5.501   Einen Klammerausdruck, dessen Glieder Sätze sind, deute ich—wenn die Reihenfolge der Glieder in der Klammer gleichgültig ist—durch ein Zeichen von der Form „$(\bar{\xi})$" an. „ξ" ist eine Variable, deren Werte die Glieder des Klammerausdruckes sind ; und der Strich über der Variablen deutet an, dass sie ihre sämtlichen Werte in der Klammer vertritt.

(Hat also ξ etwa die 3 Werte P, Q, R, so ist $(\bar{\xi}) = (P, Q, R)$.)

Die Werte der Variablen werden festgesetzt.

Die Festsetzung ist die Beschreibung der Sätze, welche die Variable vertritt.

Wie die Beschreibung der Glieder des Klammerausdruckes geschieht, ist unwesentlich.

Wir konnen drei Arten der Beschreibung unterscheiden : 1. Die direkte Aufzählung. In diesem Fall konnen wir statt der Variablen einfach ihre konstanten Werte setzen. 2. Die Angabe einer Funktion fx, deren Werte für alle Werte von x die zu beschreibenden Sätze sind. 3. Die Angabe eines formalen Gesetzes, nach welchem jene Sätze gebildet sind. In diesem Falle sind die Glieder des

5.474   The number of necessary fundamental operations depends *only* on our notation.

5.475   It is only a question of constructing a system
of signs of a definite number of dimensions—of
a definite mathematical multiplicity.

5.476   It is clear that we are not concerned here with
a *number of primitive ideas* which must be signified
but with the expression of a rule.

5.5   Every truth-function is a result of the successive
application of the operation $(- - - - -T)(\xi, \ldots.)$ to
elementary propositions.

This operation denies all the propositions in
the right-hand bracket and I call it the negation
of these propositions.

5.501   An expression in brackets whose terms are
propositions I indicate—if the order of the terms
in the bracket is indifferent—by a sign of the form
"$(\bar{\xi})$". "ξ" is a variable whose values are the
terms of the expression in brackets, and the line
over the variable indicates that it stands for all
its values in the bracket.

(Thus if ξ has the 3 values P, Q, R, then
$(\bar{\xi}) = (P, Q, R)$.)

The values of the variables must be determined.

The determination is the description of the propositions which the variable stands for.

How the description of the terms of the expression in brackets takes place is unessential.

We may distinguish 3 kinds of description :
1. Direct enumeration. In this case we can place
simply its constant values instead of the variable.
2. Giving a function fx, whose values for all
values of x are the propositions to be described.
3. Giving a formal law, according to which those
propositions are constructed. In this case the

Klammerausdrucks sämtliche Glieder einer Formenreihe.

5.502 Ich schreibe also statt „(-----W)(ξ, ...)" „N($\bar{\xi}$)".

N($\bar{\xi}$) ist die Negation sämtlicher Werte der Satzvariablen ξ.

5.503 Da sich offenbar leicht ausdrücken lässt, wie mit dieser Operation Sätze gebildet werden können und wie Sätze mit ihr nicht zu bilden sind, so muss dies auch einen exakten Ausdruck finden können.

5.51 Hat ξ nur einen Wert, so ist N($\bar{\xi}$) = $\sim$ p (nicht p), hat es zwei Werte, so ist N($\bar{\xi}$) = $\sim$ p . $\sim$ q (weder p noch q).

5.511 Wie kann die allumfassende, weltspiegelnde Logik so spezielle Haken und Manipulationen gebrauchen? Nur, indem sich alle diese zu einem unendlich feinen Netzwerk, zu dem grossen Spiegel, verknüpfen.

5.512 „ $\sim$ p" ist wahr, wenn „p" falsch ist. Also in dem wahren Satz „ $\sim$ p" ist „p" ein falscher Satz. Wie kann ihn nun der Strich „ $\sim$ " mit der Wirklichkeit zum Stimmen bringen?

Das, was in „ $\sim$ p" verneint, ist aber nicht das „ $\sim$ ", sondern dasjenige, was allen Zeichen dieser Notation, welche p verneinen, gemeinsam ist.

Also die gemeinsame Regel, nach welcher „ $\sim$ p", „ $\sim$ $\sim$ $\sim$ p", „ $\sim$ p v $\sim$ p", „ $\sim$ p . $\sim$ p", etc. etc. (ad inf.) gebildet werden. Und dies Gemeinsame spiegelt die Verneinung wieder.

5.513 Man könnte sagen : Das Gemeinsame aller Symbole, die sowohl p als q bejahen, ist der Satz „p . q". Das Gemeinsame aller Symbole, die entweder p oder q bejahen, ist der Satz „pvq".

Und so kann man sagen : Zwei Sätze sind einander entgegengesetzt, wenn sie nichts miteinander gemein haben, und : Jeder Satz hat nur ein Negativ, weil es nur einen Satz gibt, der ganz ausserhalb seiner liegt.

terms of the expression in brackets are all the terms of a formal series.

5.502   Therefore I write instead of "(- - - - - T) $(\xi, \ldots)$", "$N(\bar{\xi})$".

N $(\bar{\xi})$ is the negation of all the values of the propositional variable ξ.

5.503   As it is obviously easy to express how propositions can be constructed by means of this operation and how propositions are not to be constructed by means of it, this must be capable of exact expression.

5.51   If ξ has only one value, then N $(\bar{\xi}) = {\sim}p$ (not p), if it has two values then N $(\bar{\xi}) = {\sim}p \,.\, {\sim}q$ (neither p nor q).

5.511   How can the all-embracing logic which mirrors the world use such special catches and manipulations? Only because all these are connected into an infinitely fine network, to the great mirror.

5.512   " ${\sim}p$ " is true if "p" is false. Therefore in the true proposition " ${\sim}p$ " "p" is a false proposition. How then can the stroke " $\sim$ " bring it into agreement with reality?

That which denies in " ${\sim}p$ " is however not " $\sim$ ", but that which all signs of this notation, which deny p, have in common.

Hence the common rule according to which " ${\sim}p$ ", " $\sim \sim \sim p$ ", " ${\sim}p \,\mathrm{v}\, {\sim}p$ ", " ${\sim}p \,.\, {\sim}p$ ", etc. etc. (to infinity) are constructed. And this which is common to them all mirrors denial.

5.513   We could say : What is common to all symbols, which assert both p and q, is the proposition "$p \,.\, q$". What is common to all symbols, which assert either p or q, is the proposition "$p\mathrm{v}q$".

And similarly we can say: Two propositions are opposed to one another when they have nothing in common with one another; and every proposition has only one negative, because there is only one proposition which lies altogether outside it.

Es zeigt sich so auch in Russells Notation, dass „q : p v ~ p" dasselbe sagt wie „q" ; dass „p v ~ p" nichtssagt.

5.514 Ist eine Notation festgelegt, so gibt es in ihr eine Regel, nach der alle p verneinenden Sätz gebildet werden, eine Regel, nach der alle p bejahenden Sätze gebildet werden, eine Regel, nach der alle p oder q bejahenden Sätze gebildet werden, u. s. f. Diese Regeln sind den Symbolen äquivalent und in ihnen spiegelt sich ihr Sinn wieder.

5.515 Es muss sich an unseren Symbolen zeigen, dass das, was durch „v", „ . ", etc. miteinander verbunden ist, Sätze sein müssen.

Und dies ist auch der Fall, denn das Symbol „p" und „q" setzt ja selbst das „v", „ ~ ", etc. voraus. Wenn das Zeichen „p" in „pvq" nicht für ein komplexes Zeichen steht, dann kann es allein nicht Sinn haben ; dann können aber auch die mit „p" gleichsinnigen Zeichen „pvp", „p . p", etc. keinen Sinn haben. Wenn aber „pvp" keinen Sinn hat, dann kann auch „pvq" keinen Sinn haben.

5.5151 Muss das Zeichen des negativen Satzes mit dem Zeichen des positiven gebildet werden? Warum sollte man den negativen Satz nicht durch eine negative Tatsache ausdrücken können. (Etwa : Wenn „a" nicht in einer bestimmten Beziehung zu „b" steht, könnte das ausdrücken, dass aRb nicht der Fall ist.)

Aber auch hier ist ja der negative Satz indirekt durch den positiven gebildet.

Der positive S a t z muss die Existenz des negativen S a t z e s voraussetzen und umgekehrt.

5.52 Sind die Werte von ξ sämtliche Werte einer Funktion fx für alle Werte von x, so wird $N(\bar{\xi}) = \sim (\exists x) . fx$.

5.521 Ich trenne den Begriff Alle von der Wahrheitsfunktion.

Frege und Russell haben die Allgemeinheit in Verbindung mit dem logischen Produkt oder der

Thus in Russell's notation also it appears evident that "$q : p$ v $\sim p$" says the same as "q"; that "p v $\sim p$" says nothing.

5.514   If a notation is fixed, there is in it a rule according to which all the propositions denying p are constructed, a rule according to which all the propositions asserting p are constructed, a rule according to which all the propositions asserting p or q are constructed, and so on. These rules are equivalent to the symbols and in them their sense is mirrored.

5.515   It must be recognized in our symbols that what is connected by "v", ".", etc., must be propositions.

And this is the case, for the symbols "p" and "q" presuppose "v", "$\sim$", etc. If the sign "p" in "pvq" does not stand for a complex sign, then by itself it cannot have sense; but then also the signs "pvp", "$p.p$", etc. which have the same sense as "p" have no sense. If, however, "pvp" has no sense, then also "pvq" can have no sense.

5.5151   Must the sign of the negative proposition be constructed by means of the sign of the positive? Why should one not be able to express the negative proposition by means of a negative fact? (Like: if "a" does not stand in a certain relation to "b", it could express that aRb is not the case.)

But here also the negative proposition is indirectly constructed with the positive.

The positive *proposition* must presuppose the existence of the negative *proposition* and conversely.

5.52   If the values of ξ are the total values of a function fx for all values of x, then $N(\bar{\xi}) = \sim (\exists x) . fx$.

5.521   I separate the concept *all* from the truth-function.

Frege and Russell have introduced generality in connexion with the logical product or the logical

logischen Summe eingeführt. So wurde es schwer, die Sätze „(॑x) . fx" und „(x) . fx", in welchen beide Ideen beschlossen liegen, zu verstehen.

5.522 Das Eigentümliche der Allgemeinheitsbezeichnung ist erstens, dass sie auf ein logisches Urbild hinweist, und zweitens, dass sie Konstante hervorhebt.

5.523 Die Allgemeinheitsbezeichnung tritt als Argument auf.

5.524 Wenn die Gegenstände gegeben sind, so sind uns damit auch schon alle Gegenstände gegeben.

Wenn die Elementarsätze gegeben sind, so sind damit auch alle Elementarsätze gegeben.

5.525 Es ist unrichtig, den Satz „(॑x) . fx" — wie Russell dies tut—in Worten durch „fx ist möglich" wiederzugeben.

Gewissheit, Möglichkeit oder Unmöglichkeit einer Sachlage wird nicht durch einen Satz ausgedrückt, sondern dadurch, dass ein Ausdruck eine Tautologie, ein sinnvoller Satz, oder eine Kontradiktion ist.

Jener Präzedenzfall, auf den man sich immer berufen möchte, muss schon im Symbol selber liegen.

5.526 Man kann die Welt vollständig durch vollkommen verallgemeinerte Sätze beschreiben, das heisst also, ohne irgend einen Namen von vornherein einem bestimmten Gegenstand zuzuordnen.

Um dann auf die gewöhnliche Ausdrucksweise zu kommen, muss man einfach nach einem Ausdruck „es gibt ein und nur ein x, welches . . . ." sagen: Und dies x ist a.

5.5261 Ein vollkommen verallgemeinerter Satz ist, wie jeder andere Satz zusammengesetzt. (Dies zeigt sich daran, dass wir in „(॑x , ϕ) . ϕx" „ϕ" und „x" getrennt erwähnen müssen. Beide stehen unabhängig in bezeichnenden Beziehungen zur Welt, wie im unverallgemeinerten Satz.)

sum. Then it would be difficult to understand the propositions "$(\exists x) . fx$" and "$(x) . fx$" in which both ideas lie concealed.

5.522   That which is peculiar to the "symbolism of generality" is firstly, that it refers to a logical prototype, and secondly, that it makes constants prominent.

5.523   The generality symbol occurs as an argument.

5.524   If the objects are given, therewith are *all* objects also given.

If the elementary propositions are given, then therewith *all* elementary propositions are also given.

5.525   It is not correct to render the proposition "$(\exists x) . fx$"—as Russell does—in words "*fx* is *possible*".

Certainty, possibility or impossibility of a state of affairs are not expressed by a proposition but by the fact that an expression is a tautology, a significant proposition or a contradiction.

That precedent to which one would always appeal, must be present in the symbol itself.

5.526   One can describe the world completely by completely generalized propositions, *i.e.* without from the outset co-ordinating any name with a definite object.

In order then to arrive at the customary way of expression we need simply say after an expression "there is one and only one *x*, which . . . .": and this *x* is *a*.

5.5261   A completely generalized proposition is like every other proposition composite. (This is shown by the fact that in "$(\exists x , \phi) . \phi x$" we must mention "$\phi$" and "$x$" separately. Both stand independently in signifying relations to the world as in the ungeneralized proposition.)

Kennzeichen des zusammengesetzten Symbols: Es hat etwas mit anderen Symbolen gemeinsam.

5.5262 Es verändert ja die Wahr- oder Falschheit jedes Satzes etwas am allgemeinen Bau der Welt. Und der Spielraum, welcher ihrem Bau durch die Gesamtheit der Elementarsätze gelassen wird, ist eben derjenige, welchen die ganz allgemeinen Sätze begrenzen.

(Wenn ein Elementarsatz wahr ist, so ist damit doch jedenfalls Ein Elementarsatz mehr wahr.)

5.53 Gleichheit des Gegenstandes drücke ich durch Gleichheit des Zeichens aus, und nicht mit Hilfe eines Gleichheitszeichens. Verschiedenheit der Gegenstände durch Verschiedenheit der Zeichen.

5.5301 Dass die Identität keine Relation zwischen Gegenständen ist, leuchtet ein. Dies wird sehr klar, wenn man z. B. den Satz „$(x):fx . \supset . x = a$" betrachtet. Was dieser Satz sagt, ist einfach, dass nur a der Funktion f genügt, und nicht, dass nur solche Dinge der Funktion f genügen, welche eine gewisse Beziehung zu a haben.

Man könnte nun freilich sagen, dass eben nur a diese Beziehung zu a habe, aber um dies auszudrücken, brauchten wir das Gleichheitszeichen selber.

5.5302 Russells Definition von „$=$" genügt nicht; weil man nach ihr nicht sagen kann, dass zwei Gegenstände alle Eigenschaften gemeinsam haben. (Selbst wenn dieser Satz nie richtig ist, hat er doch Sinn.)

5.5303 Beiläufig gesprochen: Von zwei Dingen zu sagen, sie seien identisch, ist ein Unsinn, und von Einem zu sagen, es sei identisch mit sich selbst, sagt gar nichts.

5.531 Ich schreibe also nicht „$f(a,b) . a = b$", sondern „$f(a,a)$" (oder „$f(b,b)$"). Und nicht „$f(a,b) . \sim a = b$", sondern „$f(a,b)$".

5.532 Und analog: Nicht „$(\exists x,y) . f(x,y) . x = y$",

A characteristic of a composite symbol: it has something in common with *other* symbols.

5.5262   The truth or falsehood of *every* proposition alters something in the general structure of the world. And the range which is allowed to its structure by the totality of elementary propositions is exactly that which the completely general propositions delimit.

(If an elementary proposition is true, then, at any rate, there is one *more* elementary proposition true.)

5.53   Identity of the object I express by identity of the sign and not by means of a sign of identity. Difference of the objects by difference of the signs.

5.5301   That identity is not a relation between objects is obvious. This becomes very clear if, for example, one considers the proposition "$(x):fx . \supset . x=a$". What this proposition says is simply that *only* a satisfies the function f, and not that only such things satisfy the function f which have a certain relation to a.

One could of course say that in fact *only* a has this relation to a, but in order to express this we should need the sign of identity itself.

5.5302   Russell's definition of "$=$" won't do; because according to it one cannot say that two objects have all their properties in common. (Even if this proposition is never true, it is nevertheless *significant*.)

5.5303   Roughly speaking: to say of *two* things that they are identical is nonsense, and to say of *one* thing that it is identical with itself is to say nothing.

5.531   I write therefore not "$f(a,b) . a=b$", but "$f(a,a)$" (or "$f(b,b)$"). And not "$f(a,b) . \sim a=b$", but "$f(a,b)$".

5.532   And analogously: not "$(\exists x,y) . f(x,y) . x=y$",

sondern „(∃x) . f(x,x)“; und nicht „(∃x,y) . f(x,y) .
~ x = y“, sondern „(∃x,y) . f(x,y)“.

(Also statt des Russell'schen „(∃x,y) . f(x,y)“:
„(∃x,y) . f(x,y) . v . (∃x) . f(x,x)“.)

5.5321 Statt „(x) : fx ⊃ x = a“ schreiben wir also z. B.
„(∃x) . fx . ⊃ . fa : ~ (∃x,y) . fx . fy“.

Und der Satz „n u r Ein x befriedigt f( )“ lautet:
„(∃x) . fx : ~ (∃x,y) . fx . fy“.

5.533 Das Gleichheitszeichen ist also kein wesentlicher
Bestandteil der Begriffsschrift.

5.534 Und nun sehen wir, dass Scheinsätze wie:
„a = a“, „a = b . b = c . ⊃ a = c“, „(x) . x = x“, „(∃x) .
x = a“, etc. sich in einer richtigen Begriffsschrift gar
nicht hinschreiben lassen.

5.535 Damit erledigen sich auch alle Probleme, die
an solche Scheinsätze geknüpft waren.

Alle Probleme, die Russells „Axiom of Infinity“
mit sich bringt, sind schon hier zu lösen.

Das, was das Axiom of infinity sagen soll, würde
sich in der Sprache dadurch ausdrücken, dass es
unendlich viele Namen mit verschiedener Bedeutung gäbe.

5.5351 Es gibt gewisse Fälle, wo man in Versuchung
gerät, Ausdrücke von der Form „a = a“ oder „p ⊃ p“
u. dgl. zu benützen. Und zwar geschieht dies,
wenn man von dem Urbild : Satz, Ding, etc. reden
möchte. So hat Russell in den „Principles of
Mathematics“ den Unsinn „p ist ein Satz“ in Symbolen durch „p ⊃ p“ wiedergegeben und als Hypothese vor gewisse Sätze gestellt, damit deren
Argumentstellen nur von Sätzen besetzt werden
könnten.

(Es ist schon darum Unsinn, die Hypothese
p ⊃ p vor einen Satz zu stellen, um ihm Argumente
der richtigen Form zu sichern, weil die Hypothese
für einen Nicht-Satz als Argument nicht falsch,
sondern unsinnig wird, und weil der Satz selbst
durch die unrichtige Gattung von Argumenten

but "$(\exists x) . f(x,x)$"; and not "$(\exists x,y) . f(x,y) . \sim x = y$", but "$(\exists x,y) . f(x,y)$".

(Therefore instead of Russell's "$(\exists x,y) . f(x,y)$" : "$(\exists x,y) . f(x,y) . \text{v} . (\exists x) . f(x,x)$".)

5.5321   Instead of "$(x): fx \supset x = a$" we therefore write *e.g.* "$(\exists x) . fx . \supset . fa : \sim (\exists x,y) . fx . fy$".

And the proposition "*only* one x satisfies $f(\ )$" reads : "$(\exists x) . fx : \sim (\exists x,y) . fx . fy$".

5.533   The identity sign is therefore not an essential constituent of logical notation.

5.534   And we see that apparent propositions like : "$a = a$", "$a = b . b = c . \supset a = c$", "$(x) . x = x$", "$(\exists x) . x = a$", etc. cannot be written in a correct logical notation at all.

5.535   So all problems disappear which are connected with such pseudo-propositions.

This is the place to solve all the problems which arise through Russell's "Axiom of Infinity".

What the axiom of infinity is meant to say would be expressed in language by the fact that there is an infinite number of names with different meanings.

5.5351   There are certain cases in which one is tempted to use expressions of the form "$a = a$" or "$p \supset p$" As, for instance, when one would speak of the archetype Proposition, Thing, etc. So Russell in the *Principles of Mathematics* has rendered the nonsense "p is a proposition" in symbols by "$p \supset p$" and has put it as hypothesis before certain propositions to show that their places for arguments could only be occupied by propositions.

(It is nonsense to place the hypothesis $p \supset p$ before a proposition in order to ensure that its arguments have the right form, because the hypothesis for a non-proposition as argument becomes not false but meaningless, and because the proposition itself becomes senseless for argu-

unsinnig wird, also sich selbst ebenso gut, oder so schlecht, vor den unrechten Argumenten bewahrt, wie die zu diesem Zweck angehängte sinnlose Hypothese.)

5.5352 Ebenso wollte man „Es gibt keine D i n g e" ausdrücken durch „ $\sim$ ($\exists$x). x = x". Aber selbst wenn dies ein Satz wäre,—wäre er nicht auch wahr, wenn es zwar „Dinge gäbe", aber diese nicht mit sich selbst identisch wären?

5.54 In der allgemeinen Satzform kommt der Satz im Satze nur als Basis der Wahrheitsoperationen vor.

5.541 Auf den ersten Blick scheint es, als könne ein Satz in einem anderen auch auf andere Weise vorkommen.

Besonders in gewissen Satzformen der Psychologie, wie „A glaubt, dass p der Fall ist", oder „A denkt p", etc.

Hier scheint es nämlich oberflächlich, als stünde der Satz p zu einem Gegenstand A in einer Art von Relation.

(Und in der modernen Erkenntnistheorie (Russell, Moore, etc.) sind jene Sätze auch so aufgefasst worden.)

5.542 Es ist aber klar, dass „A glaubt, dass p", „A denkt p", „A sagt p" von der Form „,p' sagt p" sind: Und hier handelt es sich nicht um eine Zuordnung von einer Tatsache und einem Gegenstand, sondern um die Zuordnung von Tatsachen durch Zuordnung ihrer Gegenstände.

5.5421 Dies zeigt auch, dass die Seele—das Subjekt, etc.—wie sie in der heutigen oberflächlichen Psychologie aufgefasst wird, ein Unding ist.

Eine zusammengesetzte Seele wäre nämlich keine Seele mehr.

5.5422 Die richtige Erklärung der Form des Satzes „A urteilt p" muss zeigen, dass es unmöglich ist, einen Unsinn zu urteilen. (Russells Theorie genügt dieser Bedingung nicht.)

5.5423 Einen Komplex wahrnehmen, heisst, wahrnehmen,

ments of the wrong kind, and therefore it survives the wrong arguments no better and no worse than the senseless hypothesis attached for this purpose.)

5.5352 Similarly it was proposed to express " There are no things " by " $\sim (\exists x) . x=x$ ". But even if this were a proposition—would it not be true if indeed "There were things ", but these were not identical with themselves?

5.54 In the general propositional form, propositions occur in a proposition only as bases of the truth-operations.

5.541 At first sight it appears as if there were also a different way in which one proposition could occur in another.

Especially in certain propositional forms of psychology, like " A thinks, that p is the case ", or " A thinks p ", etc.

Here it appears superficially as if the proposition p stood to the object A in a kind of relation.

(And in modern epistemology (Russell, Moore, etc.) those propositions have been conceived in this way.)

5.542 But it is clear that " A believes that p ", " A thinks p ", " A says p ", are of the form " 'p' says p " : and here we have no co-ordination of a fact and an object, but a co-ordination of facts by means of a co-ordination of their objects.

5.5421 This shows that there is no such thing as the soul—the subject, etc.—as it is conceived in contemporary superficial psychology.

A composite soul would not be a soul any longer.

5.5422 The correct explanation of the form of the proposition " A judges p " must show that it is impossible to judge a nonsense. (Russell's theory does not satisfy this condition.)

5.5423 To perceive a complex means to perceive that

dass sich seine Bestandteile so und so zu einander verhalten.

Dies erklärt wohl auch, dass man die Figur

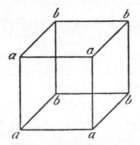

auf zweierlei Art als Würfel sehen kann ; und alle ähnlichen Erscheinungen. Denn wir sehen eben wirklich zwei verschiedene Tatsachen.

(Sehe ich erst auf die Ecken a und nur flüchtig auf b, so erscheint a vorne ; und umgekehrt.)

5.55   Wir müssen nun die Frage nach allen möglichen Formen der Elementarsätze a priori beantworten.

Der Elementarsatz besteht aus Namen.   Da wir aber die Anzahl der Namen von verschiedener Bedeutung nicht angeben können, so können wir auch nicht die Zusammensetzung des Elementarsatzes angeben.

5.551   Unser Grundsatz ist, dass jede Frage, die sich überhaupt durch die Logik entscheiden lässt, sich ohne weiteres entscheiden lassen muss.

(Und wenn wir in die Lage kommen, ein solches Problem durch Ansehen der Welt beantworten zu müssen, so zeigt dies, dass wir auf grundfalscher Fährte sind.)

5.552   Die „Erfahrung", die wir zum Verstehen der Logik brauchen, ist nicht die, dass sich etwas so und so verhält, sondern, dass etwas i s t : aber das ist eben k e i n e Erfahrung.

Die Logik ist v o r jeder Erfahrung—dass etwas s o ist.

Sie ist vor dem Wie, nicht vor dem Was.

its constituents are combined in such and such a way.

This perhaps explains that the figure

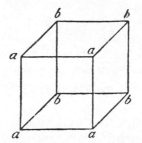

can be seen in two ways as a cube ; and all similar phenomena. For we really see two different facts.

(If I fix my eyes first on the corners *a* and only glance at *b*, *a* appears in front and *b* behind, and vice versa.)

5.55   We must now answer a priori the question as to all possible forms of the elementary propositions.

The elementary proposition consists of names. Since we cannot give the number of names with different meanings, we cannot give the composition of the elementary proposition.

5.551   Our fundamental principle is that every question which can be decided at all by logic can be decided off-hand.

(And if we get into a situation where we need to answer such a problem by looking at the world, this shows that we are on a fundamentally wrong track.)

5.552   The "experience" which we need to understand logic is not that such and such is the case, but that something *is ;* but that is *no* experience.

Logic *precedes* every experience—that something is *so.*

It is before the How, not before the What.

5.5521　Und wenn dies nicht so wäre, wie könnten wir die Logik anwenden? Man könnte sagen : Wenn es eine Logik gäbe, auch wenn es keine Welt gäbe, wie könnte es dann eine Logik geben, da es eine Welt gibt.

5.553　Russell sagte, es gäbe einfache Relationen zwischen verschiedenen Anzahlen von Dingen (Individuals). Aber zwischen welchen Anzahlen ? Und wie soll sich das entscheiden?—Durch die Erfahrung ?

(Eine ausgezeichnete Zahl gibt es nicht.)

5.554　Die Angabe jeder speziellen Form wäre vollkommen willkürlich.

5.5541　Es soll sich a priori angeben lassen, ob ich z. B. in die Lage kommen kann, etwas mit dem Zeichen einer 27-stelligen Relation bezeichnen zu müssen.

5.5542　Dürfen wir denn aber überhaupt so fragen? Können wir eine Zeichenform aufstellen und nicht wissen, ob ihr etwas entsprechen könne ?

Hat die Frage einen Sinn : Was muss s e i n, damit etwas der-Fall-sein kann ?

5.555　Es ist klar, wir haben vom Elementarsatz einen Begriff, abgesehen von seiner besonderen logischen Form.

Wo man aber Symbole nach einem System bilden kann, dort ist dieses System das logisch wichtige und nicht die einzelnen Symbole.

Und wie wäre es auch möglich, dass ich es in der Logik mit Formen zu tun hätte, die ich erfinden kann ; sondern mit dem muss ich es zu tun haben, was es mir möglich macht, sie zu erfinden.

5.556　Eine Hierarchie der Formen der Elementarsätze kann es nicht geben. Nur was wir selbst konstruieren, können wir voraussehen.

5.5561　Die empirische Realität ist begrenzt durch die Gesamtheit der Gegenstände. Die Grenze zeigt sich wieder in der Gesamtheit der Elementarsätze.

5.5521   And if this were not the case, how could
we apply logic? We could say: if there
were a logic, even if there were no world,
how then could there be a logic, since there is a
world?

5.553   Russell said that there were simple relations
between different numbers of things (individuals).
But between what numbers? And how should
this be decided—by experience?
(There is no pre-eminent number.)

5.554   The enumeration of any special forms would
be entirely arbitrary.

5.5541   How could we decide a priori whether, for
example, I can get into a situation in which I need
to symbolize with a sign of a 27-termed relation?

5.5542   May we then ask this at all? Can we set out
a sign form and not know whether anything can
correspond to it?
Has the question sense : what must there *be*
in order that anything can be the case ?

5.555   It is clear that we have a concept of the
elementary proposition apart from its special
logical form.
Where, however, we can build symbols
according to a system, there this system is the
logically important thing and not the single
symbols.
And how would it be possible that I should
have to deal with forms in logic which I can
invent: but I must have to deal with that which
makes it possible for me to invent them.

5.556   There cannot be a hierarchy of the forms of the
elementary propositions. Only that which we
ourselves construct can we foresee.

5.5561   Empirical reality is limited by the totality of
objects. The boundary appears again in the
totality of elementary propositions.

Die Hierarchien sind, und müssen unabhängig von der Realität sein.

5.5562 Wissen wir aus rein logischen Gründen, dass es Elementarsätze geben muss, dann muss es jeder wissen, der die Sätze in ihrer unanalysierten Form versteht.

5.5563 Alle Sätze unserer Umgangssprache sind tatsächlich, so wie sie sind, logisch vollkommen geordnet. —Jenes Einfachste, was wir hier angeben sollen, ist nicht ein Gleichnis der Wahrheit, sondern die volle Wahrheit selbst.

(Unsere Probleme sind nicht abstrakt, sondern vielleicht die konkretesten, die es gibt.)

5.557 Die Anwendung der Logik entscheidet darüber, welche Elementarsätze es gibt.

Was in der Anwendung liegt, kann die Logik nicht vorausnehmen.

Das ist klar: Die Logik darf mit ihrer Anwendung nicht kollidieren.

Aber die Logik muss sich mit ihrer Anwendung berühren.

Also dürfen die Logik und ihre Anwendung einander nicht übergreifen.

5.5571 Wenn ich die Elementarsätze nicht a priori angeben kann, dann muss es zu offenbarem Unsinn führen, sie angeben zu wollen.

5.6 Die Grenzen meiner Sprache bedeuten die Grenzen meiner Welt.

5.61 Die Logik erfüllt die Welt; die Grenzen der Welt sind auch ihre Grenzen.

Wir können also in der Logik nicht sagen: Das und das gibt es in der Welt, jenes nicht.

Das würde nämlich scheinbar voraussetzen, dass wir gewisse Möglichkeiten ausschliessen und dies kann nicht der Fall sein, da sonst die Logik über die Grenzen der Welt hinaus müsste; wenn sie nämlich diese Grenzen auch von der anderen Seite betrachten könnte.

The hierarchies are and must be independent of reality.

5.5562   If we know on purely logical grounds, that there must be elementary propositions, then this must be known by everyone who understands propositions in their unanalysed form.

5.5563   All propositions of our colloquial language are actually, just as they are, logically completely in order. That simple thing which we ought to give here is not a model of the truth but the complete truth itself.

(Our problems are not abstract but perhaps the most concrete that there are.)

5.557   The *application* of logic decides what elementary propositions there are.

What lies in its application logic cannot anticipate.

It is clear that logic may not conflict with its application.

But logic must have contact with its application.

Therefore logic and its application may not overlap one another.

5.5571   If I cannot give elementary propositions a priori then it must lead to obvious nonsense to try to give them.

5.6   *The limits of my language* mean the limits of my world.

5.61   Logic fills the world: the limits of the world are also its limits.

We cannot therefore say in logic: This and this there is in the world, that there is not.

For that would apparently presuppose that we exclude certain possibilities, and this cannot be the case since otherwise logic must get outside the limits of the world: that is, if it could consider these limits from the other side also.

Was wir nicht denken können, das können wir nicht denken ; wir können also auch nicht s a g e n, was wir nicht denken können.

5.62 Diese Bemerkung gibt den Schlüssel zur Entscheidung der Frage, inwieweit der Solipsismus eine Wahrheit ist.

Was der Solipsismus nämlich m e i n t, ist ganz richtig, nur lässt es sich nicht s a g e n, sondern es zeigt sich.

Dass die Welt m e i n e Welt ist, das zeigt sich darin, dass die Grenzen d e r Sprache (der Sprache, die allein ich verstehe) die Grenzen m e i n e r Welt bedeuten.

5.621 Die Welt und das Leben sind Eins.

5.63 Ich bin meine Welt. (Der Mikrokosmos.)

5.631 Das denkende, vorstellende, Subjekt gibt es nicht.

Wenn ich ein Buch schriebe „Die Welt, wie ich sie vorfand", so wäre darin auch über meinen Leib zu berichten und zu sagen, welche Glieder meinem Willen unterstehen und welche nicht etc., dies ist nämlich eine Methode, das Subjekt zu isolieren, oder vielmehr zu zeigen, dass es in einem wichtigen Sinne kein Subjekt gibt: Von ihm allein nämlich könnte in diesem Buche n i c h t die Rede sein.—

5.632 Das Subjekt gehört nicht zur Welt, sondern es ist eine Grenze der Welt.

5.633 Wo in der Welt ist ein metaphysisches Subjekt zu merken?

Du sagst, es verhält sich hier ganz, wie mit Auge und Gesichtsfeld. Aber das Auge siehst du wirklich n i c h t.

Und nichts a m G e s i c h t s f e l d lässt darauf schliessen, dass es von einem Auge gesehen wird.

5.6331 Das Gesichtsfeld hat nämlich nicht etwa eine solche Form :

What we cannot think, that we cannot think: we cannot therefore *say* what we cannot think.

5.62 This remark provides a key to the question, to what extent solipsism is a truth.

In fact what solipsism *means*, is quite correct, only it cannot be *said*, but it shows itself.

That the world is *my* world, shows itself in the fact that the limits of the language (*the* language which I understand) mean the limits of *my* world.

5.621 The world and life are one.

5.63 I am my world. (The microcosm.)

5.631 The thinking, presenting subject; there is no such thing.

If I wrote a book "The world as I found it", I should also have therein to report on my body ınd say which members obey my will and which dc not, etc. This then would be a method of isolating the subject or rather of showing that in an important sense there is no subject: that is to say, of it alone in this book mention could *not* be made.

5.632 The subject does not belong to the world but it is a limit of the world.

5.633 *Where in* the world is a metaphysical subject to be noted?

You say that this case is altogether like that of the eye and the field of sight. But you do *not* really see the eye.

And from nothing *in the field of sight* can it be concluded that it is seen from an eye.

5.6331 For the field of sight has not a form like this:

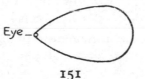

Eye —

5.634 Das hängt damit zusammen, dass kein Teil unserer Erfahrung auch a priori ist.

Alles, was wir sehen, könnte auch anders sein.

Alles, was wir überhaupt beschreiben können, könnte auch anders sein.

Es gibt keine Ordnung der Dinge a priori.

5.64 Hier sieht man, dass der Solipsismus, streng durchgeführt, mit dem reinen Realismus zusammenfällt. Das Ich des Solipsismus schrumpft zum ausdehnungslosen Punkt zusammen, und es bleibt die ihm koordinierte Realität.

5.641 Es gibt also wirklich einen Sinn, in welchem in der Philosophie nicht-psychologisch vom Ich die Rede sein kann.

Das Ich tritt in die Philosophie dadurch ein, dass die „Welt meine Welt ist“.

Das philosophische Ich ist nicht der Mensch, nicht der menschliche Körper, oder die menschliche Seele, von der die Psychologie handelt, sondern das metaphysische Subjekt, die Grenze—nicht ein Teil der Welt.

6 Die allgemeine Form der Wahrheitsfunktion ist: $[\bar{p}, \bar{\xi}, N(\bar{\xi})]$.

Dies ist die allgemeine Form des Satzes.

6.001 Dies sagt nichts anderes, als dass jeder Satz ein Resultat der successiven Anwendung der Operation $N'(\bar{\xi})$ auf die Elementarsätze ist.

6.002 Ist die allgemeine Form gegeben, wie ein Satz gebaut ist, so ist damit auch schon die allgemeine Form davon gegeben, wie aus einem Satz durch eine Operation ein anderer erzeugt werden kann.

6.01 Die allgemeine Form der Operation $\Omega'(\bar{\eta})$ ist also: $[\bar{\xi}, N(\bar{\xi})]'(\bar{\eta})\ (=[\bar{\eta}, \bar{\xi}, N(\bar{\xi})])$.

Das ist die allgemeinste Form des Überganges von einem Satz zum anderen.

5.634   This is connected with the fact that no part of our experience is also a priori.

Everything we see could also be otherwise.

Everything we can describe at all could also be otherwise.

There is no order of things a priori.

5.64   Here we see that solipsism strictly carried out coincides with pure realism. The I in solipsism shrinks to an extensionless point and there remains the reality co-ordinated with it.

5.641   There is therefore really a sense in which in philosophy we can talk of a non-psychological I.

The I occurs in philosophy through the fact that the "world is my world".

The philosophical I is not the man, not the human body or the human soul of which psychology treats, but the metaphysical subject, the limit—not a part of the world.

6   The general form of truth-function is: $[\bar{p}, \bar{\xi}, N(\bar{\xi})]$.

This is the general form of proposition.

6.001   This says nothing else than that every proposition is the result of successive applications of the operation $N'(\bar{\xi})$ to the elementary propositions.

6.002   If we are given the general form of the way in which a proposition is constructed, then thereby we are also given the general form of the way in which by an operation out of one proposition another can be created.

6.01   The general form of the operation $\Omega'(\bar{\eta})$ is therefore: $[\bar{\xi}, N(\bar{\xi})]'(\bar{\eta})\ (=[\bar{\eta}, \bar{\xi}, N(\bar{\xi})])$.

This is the most general form of transition from one proposition to another.

6.02   Und s o kommen wir zu den Zahlen: Ich definiere

$$x = \Omega^{0'} x \text{ Def. und}$$

$$\Omega'\Omega^{\nu'} x = \Omega^{\nu+1'} x \text{ Def.}$$

Nach diesen Zeichenregeln schreiben wir also die Reihe x, Ω' x, Ω' Ω' x, Ω' Ω' Ω' x, ...

so: $\Omega^{0'}$ x, $\Omega^{0+1'}$ x, $\Omega^{0+1+1'}$ x, $\Omega^{0+1+1+1'}$ x, ...

Also schreibe ich statt „[x, ξ, Ω' ξ]":

$$\text{„}[\Omega^{0'} x, \Omega^{\nu'} x, \Omega^{\nu+1'} x]".$$

Und definiere:

0 + 1 = 1 Def.

0 + 1 + 1 = 2 Def.

0 + 1 + 1 + 1 = 3 Def.

(u. s. f.)

6.021   Die Zahl ist der Exponent einer Operation.

6.022   Der Zahlbegriff ist nichts anderes, als das Gemeinsame aller Zahlen, die allgemeine Form der Zahl.

Der Zahlbegriff ist die variable Zahl.

Und der Begriff der Zahlengleichheit ist die allgemeine Form aller speziellen Zahlengleichheiten.

6.03   Die allgemeine Form der ganzen Zahl ist: [0, ξ, $\xi + 1$].

6.031   Die Theorie der Klassen ist in der Mathematik ganz überflüssig.

Dies hängt damit zusammen, dass die Allgemeinheit, welche wir in der Mathematik brauchen, nicht die z u f ä l l i g e ist.

6.1   Die Sätze der Logik sind Tautologien.

6.11   Die Sätze der Logik sagen also Nichts. (Sie sind die analytischen Sätze.)

6.111   Theorien, die einen Satz der Logik gehaltvoll erscheinen lassen, sind immer falsch. Man könnte z. B. glauben, dass die Worte „wahr" und „falsch" zwei Eigenschaften unter anderen Eigenschaften bezeichnen, und da erschiene es als eine merk-

6.02   And thus we come to numbers: I define

$$x = \Omega^{0\prime}x \text{ Def. and}$$
$$\Omega'\Omega^{\nu\prime}x = \Omega^{\nu+1\prime}x \text{ Def.}$$

According, then, to these symbolic rules we write the series $x, \Omega'x, \Omega'\Omega'x, \Omega'\Omega'\Omega'x \ldots \ldots$

as: $\Omega^{0\prime}x, \Omega^{0+1\prime}x, \Omega^{0+1+1\prime}x, \Omega^{0+1+1+1\prime}x \ldots \ldots$

Therefore I write in place of "$[x, \xi, \Omega'\xi]$",

$$\text{"}[\Omega^{0\prime}x, \Omega^{\nu\prime}x, \Omega^{\nu+1\prime}x]\text{"}.$$

And I define:
$$0 + 1 = 1 \text{ Def.}$$
$$0 + 1 + 1 = 2 \text{ Def.}$$
$$0 + 1 + 1 + 1 = 3 \text{ Def.}$$
and so on.

6.021   A number is the exponent of an operation.

6.022   The concept number is nothing else than that which is common to all numbers, the general form of number.

The concept number is the variable number.

And the concept of equality of numbers is the general form of all special equalities of numbers.

6.03   The general form of the cardinal number is: $[0, \xi, \xi+1]$.

6.031   The theory of classes is altogether superfluous in mathematics.

This is connected with the fact that the generality which we need in mathematics is not the *accidental* one.

6.1   The propositions of logic are tautologies.

6.11   The propositions of logic therefore say nothing. (They are the analytical propositions.)

6.111   Theories which make a proposition of logic appear substantial are always false. One could *e.g.* believe that the words "true" and "false" signify two properties among other properties, and then it would appear as a remarkable fact

würdige Tatsache, dass jeder Satz eine dieser Eigenschaften besitzt. Das scheint nun nichts weniger als selbstverständlich zu sein, ebensowenig selbstverständlich, wie etwa der Satz, „alle Rosen sind entweder gelb oder rot" klänge, auch wenn er wahr wäre. Ja, jener Satz bekommt nun ganz den Charakter eines naturwissenschaftlichen Satzes und dies ist das sichere Anzeichen dafür, dass er falsch aufgefasst wurde.

6.112　　Die richtige Erklärung der logischen Sätze muss ihnen eine einzigartige Stellung unter allen Sätzen geben.

6.113　　Es ist das besondere Merkmal der logischen Sätze, dass man am Symbol allein erkennen kann, dass sie wahr sind, und diese Tatsache schliesst die ganze Philosophie der Logik in sich. Und so ist es auch eine der wichtigsten Tatsachen, dass sich die Wahrheit oder Falschheit der nicht-logischen Sätze n i c h t am Satz allein erkennen lässt.

6.12　　Dass die Sätze der Logik Tautologien sind, das z e i g t die formalen — logischen — Eigenschaften der Sprache, der Welt.

Dass ihre Bestandteile s o verknüpft eine Tautologie ergeben, das charakterisiert die Logik ihrer Bestandteile.

Damit Sätze, auf bestimmte Art und Weise verknüpft, eine Tautologie ergeben, dazu müssen sie bestimmte Eigenschaften der Struktur haben. Dass sie s o verbunden eine Tautologie ergeben, zeigt also, dass sie diese Eigenschaften der Struktur besitzen.

6.1201　　Dass z. B. die Sätze „p" und „ ∼ p" in der Verbindung „ ∼ (p . ∼ p)" eine Tautologie ergeben, zeigt, dass sie einander widersprechen. Dass die Sätze „p⊃q", „p" und „q" in der Form „(p⊃q) . (p) : ⊃ : (q)" miteinander verbunden eine Tautologie ergeben, zeigt, dass q aus p und p⊃q

that every proposition possesses one of these properties. This now by no means appears self-evident, no more so than the proposition "All roses are either yellow or red" would sound even if it were true. Indeed our proposition now gets quite the character of a proposition of natural science and this is a certain symptom of its being falsely understood.

6.112 The correct explanation of logical propositions must give them a peculiar position among all propositions.

6.113 It is the characteristic mark of logical propositions that one can perceive in the symbol alone that they are true ; and this fact contains in itself the whole philosophy of logic. And so also it is one of the most important facts that the truth or falsehood of non-logical propositions can *not* be recognized from the propositions alone.

6.12 The fact that the propositions of logic are tautologies *shows* the formal—logical—properties of language, of the world.

That its constituent parts connected together *in this way* give a tautology characterizes the logic of its constituent parts.

In order that propositions connected together in a definite way may give a tautology they must have definite properties of structure. That they give a tautology when *so* connected shows therefore that they possess these properties of structure.

6.1201 That *e.g.* the propositions "p" and "$\sim p$" in the connexion "$\sim (p . \sim p)$" give a tautology shows that they contradict one another. That the propositions "$p \supset q$", "p" and "q" connected together in the form "$(p \supset q) . (p) : \supset : (q)$" give a tautology shows that q follows from p and $p \supset q$.

folgt.   Dass „(x). fx : ⊃ : fa" eine Tautologie ist, dass fa aus (x) . fx folgt. etc. etc.

6.1202   Es ist klar, dass man zu demselben Zweck statt der Tautologien auch die Kontradiktionen verwenden könnte.

6.1203   Um eine Tautologie als solche zu erkennen, kann man sich, in den Fällen, in welchen in der Tautologie keine Allgemeinheitsbezeichnung vorkommt, folgender anschaulichen Methode bedienen : Ich schreibe statt „p", „q", „r" etc. „WpF", „WqF", „WrF" etc.   Die Wahrheitskombinationen drücke ich durch Klammern aus. z. B.:

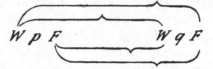

und die Zuordnung der Wahr- oder Falschheit des ganzen Satzes und der Wahrheitskombinationen der Wahrheitsargumente durch Striche auf folgende Weise :

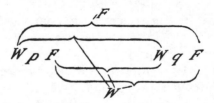

Dies Zeichen würde also z. B. den Satz p⊃q darstellen.   Nun will ich z. B. den Satz ∼ (p . ∼ p) (Gesetz des Widerspruchs) daraufhin untersuchen, ob er eine Tautologie ist.   Die Form „ ∼ ξ" wird in unserer Notation

„WξF"

That "$(x).fx:\supset:fa$" is a tautology shows that fa follows from $(x).fx$, etc. etc.

6.1202   It is clear that we could have used for this purpose contradictions instead of tautologies.

6.1203   In order to recognize a tautology as such, we can, in cases in which no sign of generality occurs in the tautology, make use of the following intuitive method: I write instead of "p", "q", "r", etc., "TpF", "TqF", "TrF", etc.   The truth-combinations I express by brackets, *e.g.* :

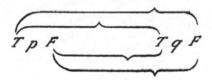

and the co-ordination of the truth or falsity of the whole proposition with the truth-combinations of the truth-arguments by lines in the following way :

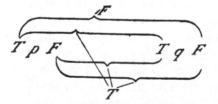

This sign, for example, would therefore present the proposition $p \supset q$.   Now I will proceed to inquire whether such a proposition as $\sim(p . \sim p)$ (The Law of Contradiction) is a tautology.   The form "$\sim\xi$" is written in our notation

"$T\xi F$"

geschrieben ; die Form „ξ . η" so :

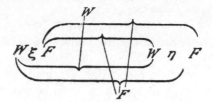

Daher lautet der Satz ~ (p . ~ q) so :

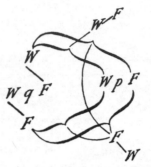

Setzen wir hier statt „q" „p" ein und untersuchen die Verbindung der äussersten W und F mit den innersten, so ergibt sich, dass die Wahrheit des ganzen Satzes a l l e n Wahrheitskombinationen seines Argumentes, seine Falschheit keiner der Wahrheitskombinationen zugeordnet ist.

6.121   Die Sätze der Logik demonstrieren die logischen Eigenschaften der Sätze, indem sie sie zu nichtssagenden Sätzen verbinden.

Diese Methode könnte man auch eine Nullmethode nennen. Im logischen Satz werden Sätze miteinander ins Gleichgewicht gebracht und der Zustand des Gleichgewichts zeigt dann an, wie diese Sätze logisch beschaffen sein müssen.

6.122   Daraus ergibt sich, dass wir auch ohne die logischen Sätze auskommen können, da wir ja in einer entsprechenden Notation die formalen Eigenschaften der Sätze durch das blosse Ansehen dieser Sätze erkennen können.

the form "$\xi . \eta$" thus :—

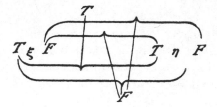

Hence the proposition $\sim (p . \sim q)$ runs thus :—

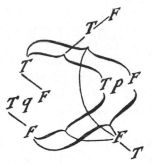

If here we put "p" instead of "q" and examine the combination of the outermost T and F with the innermost, it is seen that the truth of the whole proposition is co-ordinated with *all* the truth-combinations of its argument, its falsity with none of the truth-combinations.

6.121   The propositions of logic demonstrate the logical properties of propositions, by combining them into propositions which say nothing.

This method could be called a zero-method.   In a logical proposition propositions are brought into equilibrium with one another, and the state of equilibrium then shows how these propositions must be logically constructed.

6.122   Whence it follows that we can get on without logical propositions, for we can recognize in an adequate notation the formal properties of the propositions by mere inspection.

6.1221 Ergeben z. B. zwei Sätze „p" und „q" in der Verbindung „p⊃q" eine Tautologie, so ist kar, dass q aus p folgt.

Dass z. B. „q" aus „p⊃q . p" folgt, ersehen wir aus diesen beiden Sätzen selbst, aber wir können es auch s o zeigen, indem wir sie zu „p⊃q . p : ⊃ : q" verbinden und nun zeigen, dass dies eine Tautologie ist.

6.1222 Dies wirft ein Licht auf die Frage, warum die logischen Sätze nicht durch die Erfahrung bestätigt werden können, ebenso wenig, wie sie durch die Erfahrung widerlegt werden können. Nicht nur muss ein Satz der Logik durch keine mögliche Erfahrung widerlegt werden können, sondern er darf auch nicht durch eine solche bestätigt werden können.

6.1223 Nun wird klar, warum man oft fühlte, als wären die „logischen Wahrheiten" von uns zu „fordern": Wir können sie nämlich insofern fordern, als wir eine genügende Notation fordern können.

6.1224 Es wird jetzt auch klar, warum die Logik die Lehre von den Formen und vom Schliessen genannt wurde.

6.123 Es ist klar: Die logischen Gesetze dürfen nicht selbst wieder logischen Gesetzen unterstehen.

(Es gibt nicht, wie Russell meinte, für jede „Type" ein eigenes Gesetz des Widerspruches, sondern Eines genügt, da es auf sich selbst nicht angewendet wird.)

6.1231 Das Anzeichen des logischen Satzes ist n i c h t die Allgemeingültigkeit.

Allgemein sein, heisst ja nur: Zufälligerweise für alle Dinge gelten. Ein unverallgemeinerter Satz kann ja ebensowohl tautologisch sein, als ein verallgemeinerter.

6.1232 Die logische Allgemeingültigkeit könnte man wesentlich nennen, im Gegensatz zu jener zufälligen, etwa des Satzes „alle Menschen sind sterblich". Sätze, wie Russells „Axiom of reducibility" sind

6.1221   If for example two propositions "p" and "q" give a tautology in the connexion "$p \supset q$", then it is clear that q follows from p.

E.g. that "q" follows from "$p \supset q . p$" we see from these two propositions themselves, but we can also show it by combining them to "$p \supset q . p : \supset : q$" and then showing that this is a tautology.

6.1222   This throws light on the question why logical propositions can no more be empirically confirmed than they can be empirically refuted. Not only must a proposition of logic be incapable of being contradicted by any possible experience, but it must also be incapable of being confirmed by any such.

6.1223   It now becomes clear why we often feel as though "logical truths" must be "*postulated*" by us. We can in fact postulate them in so far as we can postulate an adequate notation.

6.1224   It also becomes clear why logic has been called the theory of forms and of inference.

6.123   It is clear that the laws of logic cannot themselves obey further logical laws.

(There is not, as Russell supposed, for every "type" a special law of contradiction ; but one is sufficient, since it is not applied to itself.)

6.1231   The mark of logical propositions is not their general validity.

To be general is only to be accidentally valid for all things. An ungeneralized proposition can be tautologous just as well as a generalized one.

6.1232   Logical general validity, we could call essential as opposed to accidental general validity, e.g. of the proposition "all men are mortal". Propositions like Russell's "axiom of reducibility" are not

nicht logische Sätze, und dies erklärt unser Gefühl : Dass sie, wenn wahr, so doch nur durch einen günstigen Zufall wahr sein könnten.

6.1233 Es lässt sich eine Welt denken, in der das Axiom of reducibility nicht gilt. Es ist aber klar, dass die Logik nichts mit der Frage zu schaffen hat, ob unsere Welt wirklich so ist oder nicht.

6.124 Die logischen Sätze beschreiben das Gerüst der Welt, oder vielmehr, sie stellen es dar. Sie „handeln" von nichts. Sie setzen voraus, dass Namen Bedeutung, und Elementarsätze Sinn haben : Und dies ist ihre Verbindung mit der Welt. Es ist klar, dass es etwas über die Welt anzeigen muss, dass gewisse Verbindungen von Symbolen—welche wesentlich einen bestimmten Charakter haben—Tautologien sind. Hierin liegt das Entscheidende. Wir sagten, manches an den Symbolen, die wir gebrauchen, wäre willkürlich, manches nicht. In der Logik drückt nur dieses aus : Dass heisst aber, in der Logik drücken nicht w i r mit Hilfe der Zeichen aus, was wir wollen, sondern in der Logik sagt die Natur der naturnotwendigen Zeichen selbst aus : Wenn wir die logische Syntax irgend einer Zeichensprache kennen, dann sind bereits alle Sätze der Logik gegeben.

6.125 Es ist möglich, und zwar auch nach der alten Auffassung der Logik, von vornherein eine Beschreibung aller „wahren" logischen Sätze zu geben.

6.1251 Darum kann es in der Logik auch n i e Überraschungen geben.

6.126 Ob ein Satz der Logik angehört, kann man berechnen, indem man die logischen Eigenschaften des S y m b o l s berechnet.

Und dies tun wir, wenn wir einen logischen Satz „beweisen". Denn, ohne uns um einen Sinn und eine Bedeutung zu kümmern, bilden wir den logischen Satz aus anderen nach blossen Z e i c h e n r e g e l n.

logical propositions, and this explains our feeling that, if true, they can only be true by a happy chance.

6.1233   We can imagine a world in which the axiom of reducibility is not valid.   But it is clear that logic has nothing to do with the question whether our world is really of this kind or not.

6.124   The logical propositions describe the scaffolding of the world, or rather they present it.   They " treat " of nothing.   They presuppose that names have meaning, and that elementary propositions have sense.   And this is their connexion with the world.   It is clear that it must show something about the world that certain combinations of symbols —which essentially have a definite character—are tautologies. Herein lies the decisive point. We said that in the symbols which we use something is arbitrary, something not.   In logic only this expresses : but this means that in logic it is not *we* who express, by means of signs, what we want, but in logic the nature of the essentially necessary signs itself asserts.   That is to say, if we know the logical syntax of any sign language, then all the propositions of logic are already given.

6.125   It is possible, also with the old conception of logic, to give at the outset a description of all " true " logical propositions.

6.1251   Hence there can *never* be surprises in logic.

6.126   Whether a proposition belongs to logic can be calculated by calculating the logical properties of the *symbol*.

And this we do when we prove a logical proposition.   For without troubling ourselves about a sense and a meaning, we form the logical propositions out of others by mere *symbolic rules*.

Der Beweis der logischen Sätze besteht darin, dass wir sie aus anderen logischen Sätzen durch successive Anwendung gewisser Operationen entstehen lassen, die aus den ersten immer wieder Tautologien erzeugen. (Und zwar folgen aus einer Tautologie nur Tautologien.)

Natürlich ist diese Art zu zeigen, dass ihre Sätze Tautologien sind, der Logik durchaus unwesentlich. Schon darum, weil die Sätze, von welchen der Beweis ausgeht, ja ohne Beweis zeigen müssen, dass sie Tautologien sind.

6.1261   In der Logik sind Prozess und Resultat äquivalent. (Darum keine Überraschung.)

6.1262   Der Beweis in der Logik ist nur ein mechanisches Hilfsmittel zum leichteren Erkennen der Tautologie, wo sie kompliziert ist.

6.1263   Es wäre ja auch zu merkwürdig, wenn man einen sinnvollen Satz logisch aus anderen beweisen könnte, und einen logischen Satz auch. Es ist von vornherein klar, dass der logische Beweis eines sinnvollen Satzes und der Beweis in der Logik zwei ganz verschiedene Dinge sein müssen.

6.1264   Der sinnvolle Satz sagt etwas aus, und sein Beweis zeigt, dass es so ist; in der Logik ist jeder Satz die Form eines Beweises.

Jeder Satz der Logik ist ein in Zeichen dargestellter modus ponens. (Und den modus ponens kann man nicht durch einen Satz ausdrücken.)

6.1265   Immer kann man die Logik so auffassen, dass jeder Satz sein eigener Beweis ist.

6.127   Alle Sätze der Logik sind gleichberechtigt, es gibt unter ihnen nicht wesentlich Grundgesetze und abgeleitete Sätze.

Jede Tautologie zeigt selbst, dass sie eine Tautologie ist.

6.1271   Es ist klar, dass die Anzahl der „logischen Grundgesetze" willkürlich ist, denn man könnte

We prove a logical proposition by creating it ·out of other logical propositions by applying in succession certain operations, which again generate tautologies out of the first. (And from a tautology only tautologies *follow*.)

Naturally this way of showing that its propositions are tautologies is quite unessential to logic. Because the propositions, from which the proof starts, must show without proof that they are tautologies.

6.1261 In logic process and result are equivalent. (Therefore no surprises.)

6.1262 Proof in logic is only a mechanical expedient to facilitate the recognition of tautology, where it is complicated.

6.1263 It would be too remarkable, if one could prove a significant proposition *logically* from another, and a logical proposition *also*. It is clear from the beginning that the logical proof of a significant proposition and the proof *in* logic must be two quite different things.

6.1264 The significant proposition asserts something, and its proof shows that it is so; in logic every proposition is the form of a proof.

Every proposition of logic is a modus ponens presented in signs. (And the modus ponens can not be expressed by a proposition.)

6.1265 Logic can always be conceived to be such that every proposition is its own proof.

6.127 All propositions of logic are of equal rank; there are not some which are essentially primitive and others deduced from these.

Every tautology itself shows that it is a tautology.

6.1271 It is clear that the number of "primitive propositions of logic" is arbitrary, for we could deduce

die Logik ja aus Einem Grundgesetz ableiten, indem man einfach z. B. aus Freges Grundgesetzen das logische Produkt bildet. (Frege würde vielleicht sagen, dass dieses Grundgesetz nun nicht mehr unmittelbar einleuchte. Aber es ist merkwürdig, dass ein so exakter Denker wie Frege sich auf den Grad des Einleuchtens als Kriterium des logischen Satzes berufen hat.)

6.13 Die Logik ist keine Lehre, sondern ein Spiegelbild der Welt.

Die Logik ist transzendental.

6.2 Die Mathematik ist eine logische Methode.

Die Sätze der Mathematik sind Gleichungen also Scheinsätze.

6.21 Der Satz der Mathematik drückt keinen Gedanken aus.

6.211 Im Leben ist es ja nie der mathematische Satz, den wir brauchen, sondern wir benützen den mathematischen Satz n u r, um aus Sätzen, welche nicht der Mathematik angehören, auf andere zu schliessen, welche gleichfalls nicht der Mathematik angehören.

(In der Philosophie führt die Frage „wozu gebrauchen wir eigentlich jenes Wort, jenen Satz" immer wieder zu wertvollen Einsichten.)

6.22 Die Logik der Welt, die die Sätze der Logik in den Tautologien zeigen, zeigt die Mathematik in den Gleichungen.

6.23 Wenn zwei Ausdrücke durch das Gleichheitszeichen verbunden werden, so heisst das, sie sind durch einander ersetzbar. Ob dies aber der Fall ist muss sich an den beiden Ausdrücken selbst zeigen.

Es charakterisiert die logische Form zweier Ausdrücke, dass sie durch einander ersetzbar sind.

6.231 Es ist eine Eigenschaft der Bejahung, dass man sie als doppelte Verneinung auffassen kann.

Es ist eine Eigenschaft von „$1+1+1+1$", dass man es als „$(1+1)+(1+1)$" auffassen kann.

logic from one primitive proposition by simply forming, for example, the logical product of Frege's primitive propositions. (Frege would perhaps say that this would no longer be immediately self-evident. But it is remarkable that so exact a thinker as Frege should have appealed to the degree of self-evidence as the criterion of a logical proposition.)

6.13   Logic is not a theory but a reflexion of the world.

Logic is transcendental.

6.2   Mathematics is a logical method.

The propositions of mathematics are equations, and therefore pseudo-propositions.

6.21   Mathematical propositions express no thoughts.

6.211   In life it is never a mathematical proposition which we need, but we use mathematical propositions *only* in order to infer from propositions which do not belong to mathematics to others which equally do not belong to mathematics.

(In philosophy the question " Why do we really use that word, that proposition?" constantly leads to valuable results.)

6.22   The logic of the world which the propositions of logic show in tautologies, mathematics shows in equations.

6.23   If two expressions are connected by the sign of equality, this means that they can be substituted for one another. But whether this is the case must show itself in the two expressions themselves.

It characterizes the logical form of two expressions, that they can be substituted for one another.

6.231   It is a property of affirmation that it can be conceived as double denial.

It is a property of " $1+1+1+1$ " that it can be conceived as " $(1+1)+(1+1)$ ".

6.232   Frege sagt, die beiden Ausdrücke haben dieselbe Bedeutung, aber verschiedenen Sinn.

Das Wesentliche an der Gleichung ist aber, dass sie nicht notwendig ist, um zu zeigen, dass die beiden Ausdrücke, die das Gleichheitszeichen verbindet, dieselbe Bedeutung haben, da sich dies aus den beiden Ausdrücken selbst ersehen lässt.

6.2321   Und, dass die Sätze der Mathematik bewiesen werden können, heisst ja nichts anderes, als dass ihre Richtigkeit einzusehen ist, ohne dass das, was sie ausdrücken, selbst mit den Tatsachen auf seine Richtigkeit hin verglichen werden muss.

6.2322   Die Identität der Bedeutung zweier Ausdrücke lässt sich nicht behaupten. Denn um etwas von ihrer Bedeutung behaupten zu können, muss ich ihre Bedeutung kennen: und indem ich ihre Bedeutung kenne, weiss ich, ob sie dasselbe oder verschiedenes bedeuten.

6.2323   Die Gleichung kennzeichnet nur den Standpunkt, von welchem ich die beiden Ausdrücke betrachte, nämlich vom Standpunkte ihrer Bedeutungsgleichheit.

6.233   Die Frage, ob man zur Lösung der mathematischen Probleme die Anschauung brauche, muss dahin beantwortet werden, dass eben die Sprache hier die nötige Anschauung liefert.

6.2331   Der Vorgang des R e c h n e n s vermittelt eben diese Anschauung.

Die Rechnung ist kein Experiment.

6.234   Die Mathematik ist eine Methode der Logik.

6.2341   Das Wesentliche der mathematischen Methode ist es, mit Gleichungen zu arbeiten. Auf dieser Methode beruht es nämlich, dass jeder Satz der Mathematik sich von selbst verstehen muss.

6.24   Die Methode der Mathematik, zu ihren Gleichungen zu kommen, ist die Substitutionsmethode.

Denn die Gleichungen drücken die Ersetzbarkeit zweier Ausdrücke aus und wir schreiten von einer

6.232　　　Frege says that these expressions have the same meaning but different senses.

But what is essential about equation is that it is not necessary in order to show that both expressions, which are connected by the sign of equality, have the same meaning : for this can be perceived from the two expressions themselves.

6.2321　　And, that the propositions of mathematics can be proved means nothing else than that their correctness can be seen without our having to compare what they express with the facts as regards correctness.

6.2322　　The identity of the meaning of two expressions cannot be *asserted*.　For in order to be able to assert anything about their meaning, I must know their meaning, and if I know their meaning, I know whether they mean the same or something different.

6.2323　　The equation characterizes only the standpoint from which I consider the two expressions, that is to say the standpoint of their equality of meaning.

6.233　　　To the question whether we need intuition for the solution of mathematical problems it must be answered that language itself here supplies the necessary intuition.

6.2331　　The process of *calculation* brings about just this intuition.

Calculation is not an experiment.

6.234　　　Mathematics is a method of logic.

6.2341　　The essential of mathematical method is working with equations.　On this method depends the fact that every proposition of mathematics must be self-evident.

6.24　　　The method by which mathematics arrives at its equations is the method of substitution.

For equations express the substitutability of two expressions, and we proceed from a number

Anzahl von Gleichungen zu neuen Gleichungen vor, indem wir, den Gleichungen entsprechend, Ausdrücke durch andere ersetzen.

6.241   So lautet der Beweis des Satzes $2 \times 2 = 4$:

$$(\Omega^\nu)^{\mu'} x = \Omega^{\nu \times \mu'} x \text{ Def.}$$

$$\Omega^{2 \times 2'} x = (\Omega^2)^{2'} x = (\Omega^2)^{1+1'} x = \Omega^{2'} \Omega^{2'} x = \Omega^{1+1'} \Omega^{1+1'} x$$
$$= (\Omega'\Omega)'(\Omega'\Omega)' x = \Omega'\Omega'\Omega'\Omega' x = \Omega^{1+1+1+1'} x = \Omega^{4'} x.$$

6.3   Die Erforschung der Logik bedeutet die Erforschung aller Gesetzmässigkeit. Und ausserhalb der Logik ist alles Zufall.

6.31   Das sogenannte Gesetz der Induktion kann jedenfalls kein logisches Gesetz sein, denn es ist offenbar ein sinnvoller Satz.—Und darum kann es auch kein Gesetz a priori sein.

6.32   Das Kausalitätsgesetz ist kein Gesetz, sondern die Form eines Gesetzes.

6.321   „Kausalitätsgesetz", das ist ein Gattungsname. Und wie es in der Mechanik, sagen wir, Minimum-Gesetze gibt,—etwa der kleinsten Wirkung—so gibt es in der Physik Kausalitätsgesetze, Gesetze von der Kausalitätsform.

6.3211   Man hat ja auch davon eine Ahnung gehabt, dass es ein „Gesetz der kleinsten Wirkung" geben müsse, ehe man genau wusste, wie es lautete. (Hier, wie immer, stellt sich das a priori Gewisse als etwas rein Logisches heraus.)

6.33   Wir glauben nicht a priori an ein Erhaltungsgesetz, sondern wir wissen a priori die Möglichkeit einer logischen Form.

6.34   Alle jene Sätze, wie der Satz vom Grunde, von der Kontinuität in der Natur, vom kleinsten Aufwande in der Natur etc. etc., alle diese sind Einsichten a priori über die mögliche Formgebung der Sätze der Wissenschaft.

6.341   Die Newtonsche Mechanik z. B. bringt die Weltbeschreibung auf eine einheitliche Form. Denken

of equations to new equations, replacing expressions by others in accordance with the equations.

6.241   Thus the proof of the proposition $2 \times 2 = 4$ runs:

$$(\Omega')^{\mu'}x = \Omega^{\nu \times \mu'}x \text{ Def.}$$

$$\Omega^{2 \times 2'}x = (\Omega^2)^{2'}x = (\Omega^2)^{1+1'}x = \Omega^{2'}\Omega^{2'}x = \Omega^{1+1'}\Omega^{1+1'}x$$
$$= (\Omega'\Omega)'(\Omega'\Omega)'x = \Omega'\Omega'\Omega'\Omega'x = \Omega^{1+1+1+1'}x = \Omega^{4'}x.$$

6.3   Logical research means the investigation of *all* *regularity*. And outside logic all is accident.

6.31   The so-called law of induction cannot in any case be a logical law, for it is obviously a significant proposition.—And therefore it cannot be a law a priori either.

6.32   The law of causality is not a law but the form of a law.*

6.321   "Law of Causality" is a class name. And as in mechanics there are, for instance, minimum-laws, such as that of least action, so in physics there are causal laws, laws of the causality form.

6.3211   Men had indeed an idea that there must be *a* "law of least action", before they knew exactly how it ran. (Here, as always, the a priori certain proves to be something purely logical.)

6.33   We do not *believe* a priori in a law of conservation, but we *know* a priori the possibility of a logical form.

6.34   All propositions, such as the law of causation, the law of continuity in nature, the law of least expenditure in nature, etc. etc., all these are a priori intuitions of possible forms of the propositions of science.

6.341   Newtonian mechanics, for example, brings the description of the universe to a unified form.

---

* *I.e.* not the form of one particular law, but of any law of a certain sort (B. R.).

wir uns eine weisse Fläche, auf der unregelmässige schwarze Flecken wären. Wir sagen nun : Was für ein Bild immer hierdurch entsteht, immer kann ich seiner Beschreibung beliebig nahe kommen, indem ich die Fläche mit einem entsprechend feinen quadratischen Netzwerk bedecke und nun von jedem Quadrat sage, dass es weiss oder schwarz ist. Ich werde auf diese Weise die Beschreibung der Fläche auf eine einheitliche Form gebracht haben. Diese Form ist beliebig, denn ich hätte mit dem gleichen Erfolge ein Netz aus dreieckigen oder sechseckigen Maschen verwenden können. Es kann sein, dass die Beschreibung mit Hilfe eines Dreiecks-Netzes einfacher geworden wäre ; das heisst, dass wir die Fläche mit einem gröberen Dreiecks-Netz genauer beschreiben könnten, als mit einem feineren quadratischen (oder umgekehrt) usw. Den verschiedenen Netzen entsprechen verschiedene Systeme der Weltbeschreibung. Die Mechanik bestimmt eine Form der Weltbeschreibung, indem sie sagt : Alle Sätze der Weltbeschreibung müssen aus einer Anzahl gegebener Sätze—den mechanischen Axiomen—auf eine gegebene Art und Weise erhalten werden. Hierdurch liefert sie die Bausteine zum Bau des wissenschaftlichen Gebäudes und sagt : Welches Gebäude immer du aufführen willst, jedes musst du irgendwie mit diesen und nur diesen Bausteinen zusammenbringen.

(Wie man mit dem Zahlensystem jede beliebige Anzahl, so muss man mit dem System der Mechanik jeden beliebigen Satz der Physik hinschreiben können.)

6.342   Und nun sehen wir die gegenseitige Stellung von Logik und Mechanik. (Man könnte das Netz auch aus verschiedenartigen Figuren etwa aus Dreiecken und Sechsecken bestehen lassen.) Dass sich ein Bild, wie das vorhin erwähnte, durch ein Netz von gegebener Form beschreiben lässt, sagt

Let us imagine a white surface with irregular black spots. We now say : Whatever kind of picture these make I can always get as near as I like to its description, if I cover the surface with a sufficiently fine square network and now say of every square that it is white or black. In this way I shall have brought the description of the surface to a unified form. This form is arbitrary, because I could have applied with equal success a net with a triangular or hexagonal mesh. It can happen that the description would have been simpler with the aid of a triangular mesh ; that is to say we might have described the surface more accurately with a triangular, and coarser, than with the finer square mesh, or vice versa, and so on. To the different networks correspond different systems of describing the world. Mechanics determine a form of description by saying : All propositions in the description of the world must be obtained in a given way from a number of given propositions—the mechanical axioms. It thus provides the bricks for building the edifice of science, and says : Whatever building thou wouldst erect, thou shalt construct it in some manner with these bricks and these alone.

(As with the system of numbers one must be able to write down any arbitrary number, so with the system of mechanics one must be able to write down any arbitrary physical proposition.)

6.342   And now we see the relative position of logic and mechanics. (We could construct the network out of figures of different kinds, as out of triangles and hexagons together.) That a picture like that instanced above can be described by a network of a given form asserts *nothing* about

175

über das Bild n i c h t s aus. (Denn dies gilt für jedes Bild dieser Art.) D a s aber charakterisiert das Bild, dass es sich durch ein bestimmtes Netz von b e s t i m m t e r Feinheit v o l l s t ä n d i g beschreiben lässt.

So auch sagt es nichts über die Welt aus, dass sie sich durch die Newtonsche Mechanik beschreiben lässt; wohl aber, dass sie sich s o durch jene beschreiben lässt, wie dies eben der Fall ist. Auch das sagt etwas über die Welt, dass sie sich durch die eine Mechanik einfacher beschreiben lässt, als durch die andere.

6.343 Die Mechanik ist ein Versuch, alle w a h r e n Sätze, die wir zur Weltbeschreibung brauchen, nach Einem Plane zu konstruieren.

6.3431 Durch den ganzen logischen Apparat hindurch sprechen die physikalischen Gesetze doch von den Gegenständen der Welt.

6.3432 Wir dürfen nicht vergessen, dass die Weltbeschreibung durch die Mechanik immer die ganz allgemeine ist. Es ist in ihr z. B. nie von b e s t i m m t e n materiellen Punkten die Rede, sondern immer nur von i r g e n d w e l c h e n.

6.35 Obwohl die Flecke in unserem Bild geometrische Figuren sind, so kann doch selbstverständlich die Geometrie gar nichts über ihre tatsächliche Form und Lage sagen. Das Netz aber ist r e i n geometrisch, alle seine Eigenschaften können a priori angegeben werden.

Gesetze, wie der Satz vom Grunde, etc., handeln vom Netz, nicht von dem, was das Netz beschreibt.

6.36 Wenn es ein Kausalitätsgesetz gäbe, so könnte es lauten: „Es gibt Naturgesetze".

Aber freilich kann man das nicht sagen: es zeigt sich.

6.361 In der Ausdrucksweise Hertz's könnte man sagen: Nur g e s e t z m ä s s i g e Zusammenhänge sind d e n k b a r.

the picture. (For this holds of every picture of this kind.) But *this* does characterize the picture, the fact, namely, that it can be *completely* described by a definite net of *definite* fineness.

So too the fact that it can be described by Newtonian mechanics asserts nothing about the world; but *this* asserts something, namely, that it can be described in that particular way in which as a matter of fact it is described. The fact, too, that it can be described more simply by one system of mechanics than by another says something about the world.

6.343　Mechanics is an attempt to construct according to a single plan all *true* propositions which we need for the description of the world.

6.3431　Through their whole logical apparatus the physical laws still speak of the objects of the world.

6.3432　We must not forget that the description of the world by mechanics is always quite general. There is, for example, never any mention of *particular* material points in it, but always only of *some points or other*.

6.35　Although the spots in our picture are geometrical figures, geometry can obviously say nothing about their actual form and position. But the network is *purely* geometrical, and all its properties can be given a priori.

Laws, like the law of causation, etc., treat of the network and not of what the network describes.

6.36　If there were a law of causality, it might run: "There are natural laws".

But that can clearly not be said: it shows itself.

6.361　In the terminology of Hertz we might say: Only *uniform* connexions are *thinkable*.

6.3611 Wir können keinen Vorgang mit dem „Ablauf der Zeit" vergleichen—diesen gibt es nicht—, sondern nur mit einem anderen Vorgang (etwa mit dem Gang des Chronometers).

Daher ist die Beschreibung des zeitlichen Verlaufs nur so möglich, dass wir uns auf einen anderen Vorgang stützen.

Ganz Analoges gilt für den Raum. Wo man z. B. sagt, es könne keines von zwei Ereignissen (die sich gegenseitig ausschliessen) eintreten, weil keine Ursache vorhanden sei, warum das eine eher als das andere eintreten solle, da handelt es sich in Wirklichkeit darum, dass man gar nicht eines der beiden Ereignisse beschreiben kann, wenn nicht irgend eine Asymmetrie vorhanden ist. Und wenn eine solche Asymmetrie vorhanden ist, so können wir diese als Ursache des Eintreffens des einen und Nicht-Eintreffens des anderen auffassen.

6.36111 Das Kant'sche Problem von der rechten und linken Hand, die man nicht zur Deckung bringen kann, besteht schon in der Ebene, ja im eindimensionalen Raum, wo die beiden kongruenten Figuren a und b auch nicht zur Deckung gebracht werden können, ohne aus diesem Raum

$$- - - \text{o} \underline{\hspace{1em}} \text{x- -x} \underline{\hspace{1em}} \text{o} - - - -$$
$$\qquad a \qquad\qquad b$$

herausbewegt zu werden. Rechte und linke Hand sind tatsächlich vollkommen kongruent. Und dass man sie nicht zur Deckung bringen kann, hat damit nichts zu tun.

Den rechten Handschuh könnte man an die linke Hand ziehen, wenn man ihn im vierdimensionalen Raum umdrehen könnte.

6.362 Was sich beschreiben lässt, das kann auch geschehen, und was das Kausalitätsgesetz ausschliessen soll, das lässt sich auch nicht beschreiben.

6.363 Der Vorgang der Induktion besteht darin, dass

6.3611   We cannot compare any process with the "passage of time"—there is no such thing—but only with another process (say, with the movement of the chronometer).

Hence the description of the temporal sequence of events is only possible if we support ourselves on another process.

It is exactly analogous for space. When, for example, we say that neither of two events (which mutually exclude one another) can occur, because there is *no cause* why the one should occur rather than the other, it is really a matter of our being unable to describe *one* of the two events unless there is some sort of asymmetry. And if there *is* such an asymmetry, we can regard this as the *cause* of the occurrence of the one and of the non-occurrence of the other.

6.36111   The Kantian problem of the right and left hand which cannot be made to cover one another already exists in the plane, and even in one-dimensional space; where the two congruent figures a and b cannot be made to cover one another without

$$- - - \circ \!\!-\!\!-\!\!-\!\!-\!\! \times \!-\!- \times \!\!-\!\!-\!\!-\!\!-\!\! \circ - - - -$$
$$ a b$$

moving them out of this space. The right and left hand are in fact completely congruent. And the fact that they cannot be made to cover one another has nothing to do with it.

A right-hand glove could be put on a left hand if it could be turned round in four-dimensional space.

6.362   What can be described can happen too, and what is excluded by the law of causality cannot be described.

6.363   The process of induction is the process of

wir das e i n f a c h s t e Gesetz annehmen, das mit unseren Erfahrungen in Einklang zu bringen ist.

6.3631 Dieser Vorgang hat aber keine logische, sondern nur eine psychologische Begründung.

Es ist klar, dass kein Grund vorhanden ist, zu glauben, es werde nun auch wirklich der einfachste Fall eintreten.

6.36311 Dass die Sonne morgen aufgehen wird, ist eine Hypothese ; und das heisst : wir w i s s e n nicht, ob sie aufgehen wird.

6.37 Einen Zwang, nach dem Eines geschehen müsste, weil etwas anderes geschehen ist, gibt es nicht. Es gibt nur eine l o g i s c h e Notwendigkeit.

6.371 Der ganzen modernen Weltanschauung liegt die Täuschung zugrunde, dass die sogenannten Naturgesetze die Erklärungen der Naturerscheinungen seien.

6.372 So bleiben sie bei den Naturgesetzen als bei etwas Unantastbarem stehen, wie die älteren bei Gott und dem Schicksal.

Und sie haben ja beide Recht, und Unrecht. Die Alten sind allerdings insofern klarer, als sie einen klaren Abschluss anerkennen, während es bei dem neuen System scheinen soll, als sei a l l e s erklärt.

6.373 Die Welt ist unabhängig von meinem Willen.

6.374 Auch wenn alles, was wir wünschen, geschähe, so wäre dies doch nur, sozusagen, eine Gnade des Schicksals, denn es ist kein l o g i s c h e r Zusammenhang zwischen Willen und Welt, der dies verbürgte, und den angenommenen physikalischen Zusammenhang könnten wir doch nicht selbst wieder wollen.

6.375 Wie es nur eine l o g i s c h e Notwendigkeit gibt, so gibt es auch nur eine l o g i s c h e Unmöglichkeit.

6.3751 Dass z. B. zwei Farben zugleich an einem Ort des Gesichtsfeldes sind, ist unmöglich und zwar logisch unmöglich, denn es ist durch die logische Struktur der Farbe ausgeschlossen.

assuming the *simplest* law that can be made to harmonize with our experience.

6.3631   This process, however, has no logical foundation but only a psychological one.

It is clear that there are no grounds for believing that the simplest course of events will really happen.

6.36311   That the sun will rise to-morrow, is an hypothesis ; and that means that we do not *know* whether it will rise.

6.37   A necessity for one thing to happen because another has happened does not exist. There is only *logical* necessity.

6.371   At the basis of the whole modern view of the world lies the illusion that the so-called laws of nature are the explanations of natural phenomena.

6.372   So people stop short at natural laws as at something unassailable, as did the ancients at God and Fate.

And they both are right and wrong. But the ancients were clearer, in so far as they recognized one clear terminus, whereas the modern system makes it appear as though *everything* were explained.

6.373   The world is independent of my will.

6.374   Even if everything we wished were to happen, this would only be, so to speak, a favour of fate, for there is no *logical* connexion between will and world, which would guarantee this, and the assumed physical connexion itself we could not again will.

6.375   As there is only a *logical* necessity, so there is only a *logical* impossibility.

6.3751   For two colours, *e.g.* to be at one place in the visual field, is impossible, logically impossible, for it is excluded by the logical structure of colour.

Denken wir daran, wie sich dieser Widerspruch in der Physik darstellt: Ungefähr so, dass ein Teilchen nicht zu gleicher Zeit zwei Geschwindigkeiten haben kann; das heisst, dass es nicht zu gleicher Zeit an zwei Orten sein kann; das heisst, dass Teilchen an verschiedenen Orten zu Einer Zeit nicht identisch sein können.

(Es ist klar, dass das logische Produkt zweier Elementarsätze weder eine Tautologie noch eine Kontradiktion sein kann. Die Aussage, dass ein Punkt des Gesichtsfeldes zu gleicher Zeit zwei verschiedene Farben hat, ist eine Kontradiktion.)

6.4   Alle Sätze sind gleichwertig.

6.41   Der Sinn der Welt muss ausserhalb ihrer liegen. In der Welt ist alles wie es ist und geschieht alles wie es geschieht; es gibt in ihr keinen Wert—und wenn es ihn gäbe, so hätte er keinen Wert.

Wenn es einen Wert gibt, der Wert hat, so muss er ausserhalb alles Geschehens und So-Seins liegen. Denn alles Geschehen und So-Sein ist zufällig.

Was es nicht-zufällig macht, kann nicht in der Welt liegen, denn sonst wäre dies wieder zufällig.

Es muss ausserhalb der Welt liegen.

6.42   Darum kann es auch keine Sätze der Ethik geben. Sätze können nichts Höheres ausdrücken.

6.421   Es ist klar, dass sich die Ethik nicht aussprechen lässt.

Die Ethik ist transzendental.

(Ethik und Aesthetik sind Eins.)

6.422   Der erste Gedanke bei der Aufstellung eines ethischen Gesetzes von der Form „du sollst . . . ." ist: Und was dann, wenn ich es nicht tue? Es ist aber klar, dass die Ethik nichts mit Strafe und Lohn im gewöhnlichen Sinne zu tun hat. Also muss diese Frage nach den Folgen einer Handlung belanglos sein.—Zum Mindesten dürfen diese Folgen nicht Ereignisse sein. Denn etwas muss doch an jener Fragestellung richtig sein. Es muss

Let us consider how this contradiction presents itself in physics. Somewhat as follows: That a particle cannot at the same time have two velocities, *i.e.* that at the same time it cannot be in two places, *i.e.* that particles in different places at the same time cannot be identical.

(It is clear that the logical product of two elementary propositions can neither be a tautology nor a contradiction. The assertion that a point in the visual field has two different colours at the same time, is a contradiction.)

6.4   All propositions are of equal value.

6.41   The sense of the world must lie outside the world. In the world everything is as it is and happens as it does happen. *In* it there is no value —and if there were, it would be of no value.

If there is a value which is of value, it must lie outside all happening and being-so. For all happening and being-so is accidental.

What makes it non-accidental cannot lie *in* the world, for otherwise this would again be accidental.

It must lie outside the world.

6.42   Hence also there can be no ethical propositions. Propositions cannot express anything higher.

6.421   It is clear that ethics cannot be expressed.

Ethics is transcendental.

(Ethics and æsthetics are one.)

6.422   The first thought in setting up an ethical law of the form "thou shalt . . ." is: And what if I do not do it? But it is clear that ethics has nothing to do with punishment and reward in the ordinary sense. This question as to the *consequences* of an action must therefore be irrelevant. At least these consequences will not be events. For there must be something right in that formulation of the question. There must be some sort

zwar eine Art von ethischem Lohn und ethischer Strafe geben, aber diese müssen in der Handlung selbst liegen.

(Und das ist auch klar, dass der Lohn etwas Angenehmes, die Strafe etwas Unangenehmes sein muss.)

6.423 Vom Willen als dem Träger des Ethischen kann nicht gesprochen werden.

Und der Wille als Phänomen interessiert nur die Psychologie.

6.43 Wenn das gute oder böse Wollen die Welt ändert, so kann es nur die Grenzen der Welt ändern, nicht die Tatsachen ; nicht das, was durch die Sprache ausgedrückt werden kann.

Kurz, die Welt muss dann dadurch überhaupt eine andere werden. Sie muss sozusagen als Ganzes abnehmen oder zunehmen.

Die Welt des Glücklichen ist eine andere als die des Unglücklichen.

6.431 Wie auch beim Tod die Welt sich nicht ändert, sondern aufhört.

6.4311 Der Tod ist kein Ereignis des Lebens. Den Tod erlebt man nicht.

Wenn man unter Ewigkeit nicht unendliche Zeitdauer, sondern Unzeitlichkeit versteht, dann lebt der ewig, der in der Gegenwart lebt.

Unser Leben ist ebenso endlos, wie unser Gesichtsfeld grenzenlos ist.

6.4312 Die zeitliche Unsterblichkeit der Seele des Menschen, das heisst also ihr ewiges Fortleben auch nach dem Tode, ist nicht nur auf keine Weise verbürgt, sondern vor allem leistet diese Annahme gar nicht das, was man immer mit ihr erreichen wollte. Wird denn dadurch ein Rätsel gelöst, dass ich ewig fortlebe ? Ist denn dieses ewige Leben dann nicht ebenso rätselhaft wie das gegenwärtige ? Die Lösung des Rätsels des Lebens in Raum und Zeit liegt a u s s e r h a l b von Raum und Zeit.

of ethical reward and ethical punishment, but this must lie in the action itself.

(And this is clear also that the reward must be something acceptable, and the punishment something unacceptable.)

6.423   Of the will as the subject of the ethical we cannot speak.

And the will as a phenomenon is only of interest to psychology.

6.43   If good or bad willing changes the world, it can only change the limits of the world, not the facts ; not the things that can be expressed in language.

In brief, the world must thereby become quite another. It must so to speak wax or wane as a whole.

The world of the happy is quite another than that of the unhappy.

6.431   As in death, too, the world does not change, but ceases.

6.4311   Death is not an event of life. Death is not lived through.

If by eternity is understood not endless temporal duration but timelessness, then he lives eternally who lives in the present.

Our life is endless in the way that our visual field is without limit.

6.4312   The temporal immortality of the human soul, that is to say, its eternal survival after death, is not only in no way guaranteed, but this assumption in the first place will not do for us what we always tried to make it do. Is a riddle solved by the fact that I survive for ever? Is this eternal life not as enigmatic as our present one? The solution of the riddle of life in space and time lies *outside* space and time.

(Nicht Probleme der Naturwissenschaft sind ja zu lösen.)

6.432 Wie die Welt ist, ist für das Höhere vollkommen gleichgültig. Gott offenbart sich nicht in der Welt.

6.4321 Die Tatsachen gehören alle nur zur Aufgabe, nicht zur Lösung.

6.44 Nicht wie die Welt ist, ist das Mystische, sondern dass sie ist.

6.45 Die Anschauung der Welt sub specie aeterni ist ihre Anschauung als—begrenztes—Ganzes.

Das Gefühl der Welt als begrenztes Ganzes ist das mystische.

6.5 Zu einer Antwort, die man nicht aussprechen kann, kann man auch die Frage nicht aussprechen.

Das Rätsel gibt es nicht.

Wenn sich eine Frage überhaupt stellen lässt, so kann sie auch beantwortet werden.

6.51 Skeptizismus ist nicht unwiderleglich, sondern offenbar unsinnig, wenn er bezweifeln will, wo nicht gefragt werden kann.

Denn Zweifel kann nur bestehen, wo eine Frage besteht; eine Frage nur, wo eine Antwort besteht, und diese nur, wo etwas gesagt werden kann.

6.52 Wir fühlen, dass selbst, wenn alle möglichen wissenschaftlichen Fragen beantwortet sind, unsere Lebensprobleme noch gar nicht berührt sind. Freilich bleibt dann eben keine Frage mehr; und eben dies ist die Antwort.

6.521 Die Lösung des Problems des Lebens merkt man am Verschwinden dieses Problems.

(Ist nicht dies der Grund, warum Menschen, denen der Sinn des Lebens nach langen Zweifeln klar wurde, warum diese dann nicht sagen konnten, worin dieser Sinn bestand.)

6.522 Es gibt allerdings Unaussprechliches. Dies zeigt sich, es ist das Mystische.

6.53 Die richtige Methode der Philosophie wäre

(It is not problems of natural science which have to be solved.)

6.432 *How* the world is, is completely indifferent for what is higher. God does not reveal himself *in* the world.

6.4321 The facts all belong only to the task and not to its performance.

6.44 Not *how* the world is, is thè mystical, but *that* it is.

6.45 The contemplation of the world sub specie aeterni is its contemplation as a limited whole.

The feeling of the world as a limited whole is the mystical feeling.

6.5 For an answer which cannot be expressed the question too cannot be expressed.

The riddle does not exist.

If a question can be put at all, then it *can* also be answered.

6.51 Scepticism is *not* irrefutable, but palpably senseless, if it would doubt where a question cannot be asked.

For doubt can only exist where there is a question ; a question only where there is an answer, and this only where something *can* be *said*.

6.52 We feel that even if *all possible* scientific questions be answered, the problems of life have still not been touched at all. Of course there is then no question left, and just this is the answer.

6.521 The solution of the problem of life is seen in the vanishing of this problem.

(Is not this the reason why men to whom after long doubting the sense of life became clear, could not then say wherein this sense consisted ?)

6.522 There is indeed the inexpressible. This *shows* itself ; it is the mystical.

6.53 The right method of philosophy would be this.

eigentlich die : Nichts zu sagen, als was sich sagen lässt, also Sätze der Naturwissenschaft—also etwas, was mit Philosophie nichts zu tun hat—, und dann immer, wenn ein anderer etwas Metaphysisches sagen wollte, ihm nachzuweisen, dass er gewissen Zeichen in seinen Sätzen keine Bedeutung gegeben hat. Diese Methode wäre für den anderen un- befriedigend—er hätte nicht das Gefühl, dass wir ihn Philosophie lehrten—aber s i e wäre die einzig streng richtige.

6.54   Meine Sätze erläutern dadurch, dass sie der, welcher mich versteht, am Ende als unsinnig erkennt, wenn er durch sie—auf ihnen—über sie hinausgestiegen ist. (Er muss sozusagen die Leiter wegwerfen, nachdem er auf ihr hinaufgestiegen ist.)

Er muss diese Sätze überwinden, dann sieht er die Welt richtig.

7   Wovon man nicht sprechen kann, darüber muss man schweigen.

To say nothing except what can be said, *i.e.* the propositions of natural science, *i.e.* something that has nothing to do with philosophy: and then always, when someone else wished to say something metaphysical, to demonstrate to him that he had given no meaning to certain signs in his propositions. This method would be unsatisfying to the other—he would not have the feeling that we were teaching him philosophy—but it would be the only strictly correct method.

6.54 My propositions are elucidatory in this way: he who understands me finally recognizes them as senseless, when he has climbed out through them, on them, over them. (He must so to speak throw away the ladder, after he has climbed up on it.)

He must surmount these propositions; then he sees the world rightly.

7 Whereof one cannot speak, thereof one must be silent.

INDEX*

(Note : Numbers in parentheses refer to paragraphs. Thus " 6.211 (2) " indicates the second paragraph of section 6.211.)

A priori
  all inference is, 5.133
  always proves to be something logical, 6.3211
  criterion of such a thought, 3.04
  geometry is, 6.35 (1)
  intuitions, scientific principles as, 6.34
  no part of experience is, 5.634
  possibility of a logical form as, 6.33
  what logic's being, consists in, 5.4731
Accident, none in logic, 2.012
Aesthetics, 6.421 (3)
Affirmation, logical property of, 6.231 (1)
Alphabet, 4.016 (2)
Ambiguity, of " property " and other words, 4.123 (3)
Analysis of propositions, 2.0201, 3.201, 3.25, 4.221 (1)
" Ambulo," a composite proposition, 4.032 (?)
Analytical propositions, 6.11
Application, successive
  defined, 5.2521 (1)
  equivalent to " and so on", 5.2523
Argument
  function cannot be its own, 3.333 (1)

places, and generality, 4.0411 (2)
Assertion
  and deducibility, 5.124 (1)
  cannot give a sense, 4.064
Assertion sign, meaningless, 4.442 (2)
Atomic facts (Sachverhalt)
  are combinations of things, 2.01, 2.03
  are mutually independent, 2.061, 2.062, 4.27 (2)
  number of combinations of, 4.27 (1)
  possible infinity of, 4.2211
  possibility of, 2.012, 2.0124
  possibility of occurrence of things in, 2.0121 (2)
  relation to elementary propositions, 4.21, 4.25
  relation to facts, 2
  relation to propositions, 4.1
  structure of, 2.032
Axiom of Infinity, 5.535 (2, 3)
Axiom of Reducibility, 6.1232, 6.1233

Brackets, their importance, 5.461

Calculation
  not an experiment, 6.2331 (2)
  of logical properties of symbols, 6.126 (1)

* The Editor is indebted to Professor Max Black for providing this Index, which was originally prepared for the use of his students at Cornell University.

Case, the (*der Fall*)
  and substance, 2.024
  and the world, 1
  equated with fact, 2
  is existence of atomic facts, 2
Causality : no causal nexus,
  5.136, 5.1361
Causality, law of
  as limit of the describable,
    6.362
  cannot be said, 6.36 (2)
  is form of a law, 6.32, 6.321,
    6.361
Certainty
  as limiting case of probability,
    5.152 (3)
  of truth of tautology, 4.464 (1)
  opposed to possibility and im-
    possibility, 4.464 (2)
Clarity : everything can be said
  and thought clearly, 4.116
Classes, theory of, superfluous in
  mathematics, 6.031 (1)
Colloquial language. *See* Ordinary language
Colour
  a form of objects, 2.0251
  logical structure of, 6.3751
" Complex," a formal concept,
  4.1272 (7, 8)
Complexes
  and definition, 3.24 (4)
  given only by descriptions,
    3.24 (2)
  how perceived, 5.5423
  propositions about, in internal
    relation to a statement
    about constituents,
    3.24 (1)
  statements about, analysable,
    2.0201
Configuration of objects, 2.0272,
  3.21. (*See also* Structure)
Constant : expression as,
  3.312 (2)
Contradiction. (*See also* Denial)
  defined, 4.46 (4)

limiting case of combination of
  symbols, 4.466 (4)
not a picture of reality, 4.462
shared by propositions, 5.143
Correspondence
  between objects and picture
    elements, 2.13
  of configuration of simple signs
    and objects, 3.21

Darwinian theory, irrelevant to
  philosophy, 4.1122
Death, 6.431, 6.4311
Deducibility
  and identity, 5.141
  and obviousness, 5.1363
  and relative content, 5.14
  and structure, 5.13
  relation to form, illustrated,
    5.1311 (1)
Definition
  as analysis, 3.26
  as rule of translation, 3.343
  effect upon signification,
    3.261 (1)
  how symbolized, 4.241 (3)
  of a symbol for a complex,
    3.24 (4)
  of ' complete analysis ' (of
    proposition), 3.201
  of ' contradiction ', 4.46 (4)
  of ' expression ', 3.31 (1)
  of ' feature ', 4.1221
  of ' form ', 2.033
  of ' form of an object ', 2.0141
  of ' form of representation ',
    2.151
  of ' formal concept ', 4.126 (1)
  of ' formal series ', 4.1252 (1)
  of ' independent propositions ',
    5.152 (1)
  of ' logical picture ', 2.181
  of ' logical place ', 3.41
  of ' measure of probability ',
    5.15
  of ' name ', 3.202

of ' negation ' (in sense of simultaneous denial), 5.5
of ' number ', 6.022 (2)
of numbers, 6.02
of 'operation ', 5.23
of ' propositional sign ', 3.12
of ' propositional variable ', 3.313 (3)
of ' range ', 4.463
of ' sign ', 3.32
of ' simple sign ', 3.201
of ' structure ' (of atomic facts) 2.032
of ' successive application ', 5.2521 (1)
of ' successor ', 4.1252 (4)
of ' tautology ', 4.46 (4)
of ' truth-grounds ', 5.101 (2)
of ' truth-operations ', 5.234
of ' truth-possibilities ', 4.3
only an expedient in presentation, 4.242
rules for, 5.451 (2)
Denial
as determining logical place, 4.0641
by means of what is common to all negation symbols, 5.512 (2)
is an operation, 5.2341 (2)
needs a single definition, 5.451
possibility of, presupposed in affirmation, 5.44 (4)
occurrence of, does not characterize sense, 4.0621 (2)
reverses sense, 5.2341 (3)
Denial, sign of
corresponds to nothing in reality, 4.0621
does not refer to an object, 5.44 (5)
Description
of a fact by a proposition, 4.023 (3)
of an object, 4.023 (4)
of complex, 3.24 (2)
of expressions, 3.33
of propositions, 3.317 (2)
of reality by a proposition, 4.023 (2)
of states of affairs, 3.144
of the world
Descriptions, systems of, 6.341
Distinguishability, 2.02331
" Dynamic models", 4.04 (2)

Ego, the non-psychological, 5.641
Elucidation of primitive signs, 3.263
Equality, meaning of sign of, 6.23 (1)
Equations
as expressing substitutability, 6.24 (2)
characterize a standpoint, 6.2323
not needed to express synonymity, 6.232 (2)
Equiprobability, 5.154 (3)
Essence
and general form of proposition, 5.471
of notation, 3.342
of pictorial nature, 4.013
of propositions, 3.341, 4.027, 4.03, 4.016, 4.5 (2), 5.471
of representation, 4.016
of symbol, 3.341, 3.343, 4.465
of the world, 5.4711
Essential property, of a thing, to be a possible constituent of atomic fact, 2.011
Eternity, 6.4311
Ethics, 6.421, 6.422
Existence
of atomic facts, 2.11, 4.1
of logical place, 3.4
Expedients, in logic, 5.452
Exponent, of an operation, 6.021
Expressions
all that need to be translated, 4.025 (1)

Expressions—*continued*
guarantee existence of the logical place, 3.4
have meaning only in a proposition, 3.314 (1)
presented by a variable, 3.313 (1)
the proposition is a function of them, 3.318
the term defined, 3.31 (1)
External property, 2.01231, 2.0233. (*See also* Internal property)

"Fact", a formal concept, 4.1272 (7, 8)
Facts (*Tatsache*). (*See also* States of affairs *and* Atomic facts)
and pictures, 2.1, 2.11
compose the world, 1.1, 1.2
existence of, 2
mutual independence of, 1.21
negative, 2.06 (2)
required for expression of sense, 3.142
the world divides into, 1.2
totality of, 1.11
Fate, and the ancients, 6.372 (1)
Feature, explained, 4.1221
Features of symbols, express formal properties, 4.125 (6)
Form. (*See also* Possibility)
and possibility of structure, 2.033
and substance, 2.025
cannot be said to have properties, 4.1241
general, of propositions, 4.5, 5.47
general propositional, and truth operations, 5.54
is a variable, 4.53
logical, 2.18. (*See also* Prototype)
and variable, 3.315

cannot be represented in proposition, 4.12, 4.121 (1)
how determined by a sign, 3.327
of propositions, 4.0031
of a spot, 4.063
of expressions, 3.31 (4)
shown by substitutability, 6.23 (2)
of functions, 3.333 (2)
of objects, 2.0141, 2.0233, 2.0251
of propositions, 3.311
of reality, 2.18
of representation
defined, 2.151
function of, in pictures, 2.22
is shown forth, 2.172
of the world consists of objects 2.022-3
of values of a variable, 4.1271 (2)
Formal, equated with logical 6.12 (1)
Formal concept
already given with object to which it applies, 4.12721
as primitive idea, 4.12721
characteristics of, 4.126 (5, 7)
defined, 4.126 (1)
examples of, 4.1272 (7, 8)
expressed by variables, 4.126 (8), 4.127
opposed to "proper" concept, 4.126 (2)
questions about existence of, senseless, 4.127
Formal law, as determining formal series, 5.501 (6)
Formal properties
connexion with structure, 5.321
explained, 4.122 (1)
expressed by features of symbols, 4.126 (6)
Formal series
defined, 4.1252 (1)

example of, 4.45 (2)

expression for general term of, 5.2522

general term of, 4.1273 (2)

needs variables, 4.1273

of truth functions, 5.1 (1)

progress from term to term of, 5.252

Freedom of the will, 5.1362 (1)

Frege, 3.143, 3.318, 3.325, 4.063 (1), 4.1272 (8), 4.1273, 4.4431, 5.02 (3), 5.132 (4), 5.42, 5.451, 5.4733 (1), 5.521, 6.1271, 6.232 (1)

Frequency, of occurrence of events, 5.154 (1)

" Function ", a formal concept, 4.1273 (7, 8)

Function

and composition, 5.47 (3)

cannot be its own argument, 3.333, 5.251

cannot present formal concepts, 4.126 (4)

distinct from operation, 5.25 (3)

elementary proposition is a, of names 4.24 (2)

proposition is a, of names, 3.318, 4.24 (2)

Future, no knowledge of, 6.26311

Generality

accidental, 6.031 (2), 6.1232

concept of, separated from truth-function, 5.521

essential

needed in mathematics, 6.031 (2)

opposed to accidental generality, 6.1232

how shown, 5.1311 (2)

how symbolized, 4.0411

its notation contains a proto-type, 3.24 (3), 5.522

symbol for, occurs as an argument, 5.523

symbolism for, makes constants prominent, 5.522

refers to logical prototype, 5.522

Geometrical place, and possibility, 3.411

Geometry, as a priori, 6.35 (1)

God, 6.432, 6.372 (1)

" Green is green ", 3.323 (3)

Hertz, 4.04 (2), 6.361

Hieroglyphic writing, 4.106

Idealists, their explanation of seeing spatial relations, 4.0412

Identity

cannot be asserted, 6.2322

criticism of Russell's definition of, 5.5302

how expressed, 5.53, 5.531, 5.532, 5.5321

not a property, 5.473 (2)

not a relation between objects, 5.5301 (1)

of sign-tokens, 3.203

sign of

dispensable, 5.533, 6.232 (2)

its meaning, 4.241 (2)

Immortality, 6.4312 (1)

Inconceivability, and internality of properties, 4.123

Independence, of propositions, defined, 5.152 (1)

Index (of a name)

explained, 5.02

confused with argument, 5.02 (3)

Induction

as assumption of simplicity, 6.363

has only psychological foundation, 6.3631 (1)

INDEX

Induction, law of
  not a logical law, 6.31
  not a priori, 6.31
Inference
  is a priori, 5.133
  " Laws of ", senseless, 5.132(4)
Internal properties. (*See also* Formal properties)
  and features, 4.1221
  and inconceivability, 4.123 (1)
  and structure, 4.122 (2)
  knowledge of, needed for knowledge of objects, 2.01231
  of a proposition, describe reality, 4.023 (4)
  of possible states of affairs, 4.124 (1), 4.125
  their holding is shown, 4.122(4)
Internal relations
  and deducibility, 5.131
  and definition of formal series, 4.1252 (1)
  between structures of propositions, 5.2
  equivalent to operations, 5.232
  of statement about a complex to a statement about constituents, 3.24 (1)
  representation as an instance, 4.014 (1)
Internal similarity, 4.0141
" Is," meanings of, 3.323 (2)

Language (*See also* Ordinary Language)
  able to express every sense, 4.022 (1)
  as supplying intuition, 6.233
  " critique of ", 4.0031
  disguises the thought, 4.002 (4)
  is totality of propositions, 4.001
  limits of my, 5.6
  logic of, 4.002 (3), 4.003 (1)
  translation of, 3.343
Law of least action, 6.3211

Laws of nature, not explanations, 6.371
Life, the problem of, 6.52, 6.521
Logic. (*See also* Logical propositions)
  all is accident outside, 6.3
  all questions of, answerable off-hand, 5.551 (1)
  and mechanics, 6.342
  application of, 5.5521, 5.557
  as all-embracing, world reflecting, 5.511
  calculation in, 6.121 (1)
  cannot cross limits of world, 5.61 (3)
  deals with possibilities, 2.0121 (3), 5.555 (3)
  every proposition of, its own proof, 6.1265
  expedients in, 5.452, 5.511
  impossibility of " contradicting ", 3.03-3.032, 5.4731
  impossibility of describing the world in, 5.61 (2)
  irrelevance of monism and dualism to, 4.128 (2)
  is a priori, 5.4541 (2), 5.4731, 5.551 (1)
  is transcendental, 6.13 (2)
  its propositions are tautologies, 6.1, 6.22
  laws of, do not obey further laws, 6.123 (1)
  must take care of itself, 5.454 (1)
  no classification in, 5.454 (1)
  no mistakes possible in, 5.473 (3)
  no numbers in, 5.453 (2)
  no primitive propositions in, 6.127 (1)
  no surprises in, 6.1251
  not a natural science, 6.111
  not a theory, 6.13 (1)
  nothing accidental in, 2.012
  of constituents, shown by tautologies, 6.12 (2)

of facts, cannot be ִrepresented, 4.0312 (2)

possibility in, 5.473 (2)

precedes every experience, 5.552 (2)

" primitive propositions " of, arbitrary in number, 6.1271

problems of, concrete, 5.5563 (2)

process and result equivalent in, 6.1261

proof in, 6.126 (2-4), 6.1262

propositions of, say nothing, 5.43 (2)

reflects the world, 6.13 (1)

role of postulation in, 6.1223

searches for regularity, 6.3

simplicity of, 5.4541

whole philosophy of, 6.113

why called theory of forms, 6.1224

" zero-method " in, 6.121 (2)

Logical, equated with formal, 6.12 (1)

Logical constants

disappearance of, 5.441

do not represent, 4.0312 (2)

only one of them, 5.47 (4), 5.472

there are none, 5.4

Logical coordinates, as determining logical place, 3.41

Logical forms, are anumerical, 4.128 (1)

Logical grammar, 3.325 (1) (See also Logical syntax)

" Logical objects ", there are no, 4.441, 5.4

Logical place (See also Logical space)

denial as determining, 4.0641

proposition determines one, 3.42 (1)

relation to propositional sign and logical coordinates, 3.41

Logical properties of propositions, demonstrated by producing tautologies, 6.121

Logical propositions

as forms of a proof, 6.1264 (1)

as modus ponens, 6.1264 (2)

connection with the world of, 6.124

dispensable, 6.122

have a peculiar place among all propositions, 6.112

have equal rank, 6.127 (1)

not confirmable by experience, 6.1222

not distinguished by generality, 6.1231 (1)

present the scaffolding of the world, 6.124

their truth discernible in the symbol, 6.113

" treat " of nothing, 6.124

Logical space (See also Logical place)

and the world, 1.13

everything is in, 2.013

facts in, 1.13

given with every proposition, 3.42 (1)

pictures present facts in, 2.11, 2.202

place in, determined by proposition, 3.4

Logical syntax

and rules of translation, 3.344

implies all logical propositions, 6.124

meanings of signs plays no role in, 3.33

need for obeying, 3.325 (1)

rules of, 3.334

Mathematics

has no need for theory of classes, 6.031 (1)

intuition in, place of, 6.233

is a logical method 6.2 (1), 6.234

Mathematics—*continued*
  method of, working with equations, 6.2341
  no accidental generality in, 6.031 (2)
  proof in, significance of, 6.2321
  propositions of
    all self-evident, 6.2341
    are equations, 6.2 (2)
    as links in inference, 6.211
    express no thoughts, 6.21
    show logic of the world, 6.22
  uses method of substitution, 6.24 (1)
Mauthner, 4.0031
Mechanics
  its generality, 6.3432
  nature of, 6.343
  relation to logic, 6.342
Microcosm, the, 5.63
Meaning
  of names, 3.3
  of primitive signs, 3.263
Modus Ponens, 6.1264 (2)
Multiplicity
  and number of dimensions of signs, 5.474
  and symbol for generality, 4.0411 (3)
  cannot be represented, 4.041
  the same in the proposition and the state of affairs represented, 4.04
Mystical, the, 6.44, 6.45, 6.522

Names
  are primitive signs, 3.26
  are simple signs, 3.202
  are simple symbols, 4.24 (1)
  are unanalysable, 3.26
  cannot be defined, 3.261 (2)
  cannot express sense, 3.142
  dispensable in describing the world, 5.526
  elementary proposition a connexion of, 4.22
  have meaning only in context of proposition, 3.3
  how they occur in propositions, 4.23
  index of, 5.02 (1)
  no composition essential, 3.3411
  resemble points, 3.144 (2)
  the " real ", 3.3411
  variable, 3.314 (2)
Natural sciences
  are the totality of true propositions, 4.11
  do not include philosophy, 4.111
Necessity : only *logical* necessity, 6.37
Negation (*See* Denial)
Negation (=Simultaneous denial)
  introduced, 5.5
  symbolized, 5.502
Newtonian mechanics, 6.341, 6.342 (2)
Nonsense (*Unsinn*)
  examples of, 5.5303, 5.5351 (2)
  impossible to judge, 5.5422
Nonsensical, logical propositions not, 4.4611
Notation (*See also* Language)
  arbitrariness of, 3.342
  essence of, 3.342
" Number ", a formal concept, 4.1272 (7, 8)
Number
  concept of, 6.022
  concept of equality of, 6.1022 (3)
  general form of, 6.022 (1), 6.03
Numbers
  as exponents of operation, 6.021
  definitions of, 6.02
  ordered by internal relation, 4.1252 (2)

" Object ", a pseudo-concept, 4.1272 (1)

Objects
  and possibility, 2.014
  are colourless, 2.0232
  are referred to by names,
    3.203, 3.22
  are simple, 2.02
  are substance of world, 2.021
  are the fixed form of the
    world, 2.023, 2.026
  as determining bounds of em-
    pirical reality, 5.5561 (1)
  can only be named, 3.221
  cannot be asserted, 3.221
  common characteristics of, not
    shown by similarity of
    signs, 3.322
  configuration of, 3.21
  form of, 2.0141
  if given, *all* are given, 5.524 (1)
  independence of, 2.0122
  occurrence in atomic facts of,
    2.012-2.0123
  possible infinity of, 4.2211
  possibility of connexion with
    other objects, 2.0121 (4)
  senseless to speak of their
    existence, 4.1272 (5)
  senseless to speak of their
    number, 4.1272 (6)
Obviousness, and deducibility,
  5.1363
Occam's razor, 3.328, 5.47321 (1)
Operations
  assert nothing, 5.25 (2)
  basis of, 5.21, 5.24 (3), 5.25 (2),
    5.251
  can cancel out, 5.253, 5.254
  characterize difference in
    forms, 5.24 (a), 5.241
  connexion with structure, 5.22,
    6.002
  defined, 5.23
  depend upon formal proper-
    ties, 5.231
  distinct from functions,
    5.25 (3)
  examples of, 5.2341 (2)

  exponent of, 6.021
  not relations, 5.42 (1)
  number of basic, depends only
    on our notation, 5.474
  occurrence of, does not char-
    acterize sense, 5.25 (1)
  result of, can be basis of same
    operations, 5.251
  shown in a variable, 5.24 (1)
  signs for, are punctuations,
    5.4611
  successive application of,
    5.2521, 5.2523
Ordinary language
  all its propositions completely
    in order, 5.5563
  ambiguity of, 3.323
  as complicated as the human
    organism, 4.002 (2)
  needs complicated adjust-
    ments, 4.002 (5)

Philosophy
  an activity, not a theory,
    4.112 (2)
  and the Darwinian theory,
    4.1122
  danger of confusion with psy-
    chology, 4.1121 (3)
  demarcates natural science,
    4.113
  demarcates the thinkable,
    4.114
  displays the speakable, 4.115
  importance of possibility in,
    3.3421
  in no special relation to psy-
    chology, 4.1121 (1)
  is full of confusions, 3.324
  its object the logical clarifica-
    tion of thoughts, 4.112 (1)
  makes propositions clear,
    4.112 (4)
  mostly consists of senseless
    statements, 4.003
  not a natural science, 4.111
  results in elucidations, 4.112(3)

Philosophy—*continued*
  right method of, 6.53
  value of questions about pur-
    pose of symbolism in,
    6.211 (1)
Physical laws, refer to objects of
  the world, 6.3431
Pictures
  and logical space, 2.11
  are compared with reality,
    2.223
  are facts, 2.14, 2.141
  are models of reality, 2.12, 4.01
  form of representation of, 2.15
  have form of representation in
    common with reality, 2.16,
    2.171
  how linked with reality, 2.151,
    2.1511, 2.201, 2.21
  include representing relation,
    2.1513
  logical
    are thoughts, 3.
    propositions as, 4.03 (3)
    the term defined, 2.181
  made by us, 2.1
  none a priori true, 2.224, 2.225
  possibility of, requires sub-
    stance, 2.0212
  propositions are, 4.012
  propositions as, of reality,
    4.021
  represent their sense, 2.221
Possibility, 2.0122-3
  and conceivability, 3.02
  and form of representation,
    2.151
  and logic, 2.0121 (3), 5.473 (2)
  and logical place, 3.411
  and nature of the world, 3.3421
  of atomic facts, 2.012, 2.0124
  of connexion of things,
    2.0121 (4)
  of method of symbolizing,
    3.3421
  of projection, 3.13 (2)
  of propositions, 4.0312 (1)

of states of affairs, 2.014, 2.202,
    2.203
  how shown, 5.525 (2)
  of structure is form, 2.033
" Postulation " of " logical
    truths ", 6.1223
Primitive ideas, formal concepts
    as, 4.12721
Primitive signs
  how their meanings are eluci-
    dated, 3.263
  names are, 3.26
  of logic
    as forms of combination, 5.46
    need to be justified, 5.45
    rules of definition apply to,
      5.451 (2)
  signify differently from non-
    primitive signs, 3.261 (2)
Principles, scientific, as a priori
    intuitions, 6.34
Probability
  based on series of truth-
    functions, 5.1
  does not apply to isolated pro-
    positions, 5.153
  has certainty as a limiting case
    of, 5.152 (3)
  involves general description of
    propositional form,
    5.156 (2)
  is a generalization, 5.156 (1)
  measure of, defined, 5.15, 5.151
  needed in default of certainty,
    5.156 (2)
  of elementary propositions,
    5.152 (2)
  proposition
    an extract from other pro-
      positions, 5.156 (5)
    has no special object, 5.1511
    relation of experience to,
      5.154 (4)
    relation to certainty, possi-
      bility, impossibility,
      4.464 (2)
    unit of, 5.155

INDEX

Problems, the deepest, are no problems, 4.003 (3)

Projection
and translation, 4.0141
method of, as thought, 3.11 (2)
possibility of, belongs to proposition, 3.13 (2)

Proof
in logic, a mechanical expedient, 6.1263
of significant proposition contrasted with proof in logic, 6.1263
of twice two, 6.241

Propositional connexion (*Satzverband*), 4.221

Propositional sign
as determining logical place, 3.41
cannot contain itself, 3.332
defined, 3.12
elements of, 3.2
essential nature of, 3.1431 (1)
is a fact, 3.14, 3.143
relation of, to proposition, 3.12
sense of, needs no explanation, 4.02, 4.021
truth table as, 4.44, 4.442 (1)

Propositional variable
bar symbol for, 5.501
defined, 3.313 (3)
determination of values of, 3.316
expresses a formal concept, 4.126 (8)
every variable conceivable as, 3.314
relation to logical form, 3.315

Propositions
accidental features of, 3.34
about complexes, 3.24
all of equal value, 6.4
always complete pictures, 5.156 (4)
analysis of, 3.201, 3.25, 4.221 (1)

and truth possibilities of elementary prepositions, 4.4
are articulated, 3.141 (2), 3.251, 4.032 (1)
are compared with reality, 4.05
are composite, 4.032 (2), 5.5261 (1)
are descriptions of facts, 4.023 (3)
are expressions, 3.31 (2)
are expressions of their truth conditions, 4.431 (2)
are generalizations of elementary propositions, 4.52
are pictures of reality, 4.021
are truth-functions of elementary propositions, 5(1)
as configurations of objects, 2.0231
as functions of expressions, 3.318
as logical pictures, 4.01 (1), 4.03 (3)
as models of reality, 4.01 (2)
can say nothing about themselves, 3.332
cannot assert their own truth, 4.442 (3)
cannot be given sense by assertion, 4.064
cannot represent logical form, 4.12 (1), 4.121
completely generalized, 5.526 (1), 5.5261 (1)
content of, 3.13 (4)
denial of, 4.0641
determine one logical place each, 3.42
elementary
are truth-arguments of proposition, 5.01
assignment of truth-values to, describes the world, 4.26
cannot be given a priori, 5.5571

201

Propositions—*continued*

cannot contradict other elementary propositions, 4.211

composition of, cannot be given, 5.55 (2)

concept of, 5.555 (1)

consist of names, 4.22, 5.55 (2)

contain all logical operations, 5.47 (2)

forms of, no hierarchy of, 5.556

if given, *all* are given, 5.524 (2)

importance of, for understanding other propositions, 4.411

how symbolized, 4.24 (2, 3)

logically independent, 5.134

possible forms of, 5.55

purely logical grounds for there being, 5.5562

range allowed by, 5.5262 (1)

relation of truth possibilities of, to other propositions, 4.4

relation to atomic facts, 4.21, 4.25

relation to tautology and contradiction, 6.3751(3)

essential features of, 3.34

expression of thoughts in, 3.2

follow from elementary propositions, 4.52

general form of, 5.47 (5)

have elementary propositions as truth-arguments, 5.01

have sense independent of facts, 4.061

have truth-value because pictures of reality, 4.06

how understood, 4.024

in them names stand for objects, 3.22

logical (*See* Logical propositions)

logical form of, 4.0031

most general form of, 4.5, 6

need only ' yes ' or ' no ' to fix reality, 4.023 (1)

neither probable nor improbable in themselves, 5.153

number of possibilities of agreement with truth-possibilities of elementary propositions, 4.42, 4.45 (1)

opposition of, 5.513 (2)

present existence and non-existence of atomic facts, 4.1

presuppositions of, 5.5151 (3)

" primitive ", 5.43 (1)

probability, have no special object, 5.1511

psychological, 5.541, 5.542

reach through whole logical space, 3.42 (3)

relation of, to propositional sign, 3.12

resemble arrows, 3.144 (2)

say how, not what a thing is, 3.221

sense of, unchanged by adjoining tautology, 4.465

show their sense, 4.022

show what they say, 4.461 (1)

significant
are thoughts, 4
content of, 3.13 (4, 5)

what is common to, illustrated, 5.513 (1)

what they say, 4.022 (2)

what logical space given with, 3.42 (1)

Prototype

and logical form, 3.315

and symbolism for generality, 5.522

and variable, 3.315

examples of, 3.333 (1), 5.5351 (1)

in notation for generality, 3.24 (3), 5.522

INDEX

Pseudo-concept, 4.1272 (1)
proposition and *thing* as,
5.5351 (1)
Pseudo-propositions, 5.535 (1)
arising from use of pseudo-
concepts, 4.1272 (4)
mathematical propositions are,
6.2 (2)
Psychology, and philosophy,
4.1121

Range, defined, 4.463
Reality
as existence of atomic facts,
2.06 (1)
completely described by proposition, 4.023 (2)
described by internal properties of proposition,
4.023 (4)
empirical, bounded by totality
of objects, 5.5561 (1)
form of, 2.18
how linked to pictures, 2.1511-
2.15121
logical features of, 4.023 (5)
not pictured by tautology or
contradiction, 4.462
pictures are models of, 2.12
pictures compared with, 2.21,
2.223
proposition as picture of,
4.01 (1), 4.021
propositions are compared
with, 4.05
total, is the world, 2.063
Representation, logic of, 4.015
(*See also* Form of representation)
Representing relation, belongs to
the picture, 2.1513
Right and left hand, Kantian
problem of, 6.36111
Rules, as equivalent to symbols,
5.514
Russell, 3.318, 3.325, 3.331, 3.333
4.0031, 4.12721, 4.1272 (8),
4.1273, 4.241 (3), 5.02 (2),
5.132 (4), 5.252, 5.4, 5.42,
5.452 (2), 5.513 (3), 5.521,
5.525, 5.5302, 5.535, 5.541
(4), 5.5422, 5.553 (1), 6.123
(2), 6.1232
Russell's paradox, 3.333 (4)

Saying
by propositions, 4.022 (2)
impossibility of, what we cannot think, 5.61 (4)
Scaffolding, logical, 3.42 (3),
4.023 (5), 6.124
Scepticism, 6.51 (1)
Self-evidence (*See also* Obviousness)
how discarded in logic, 5.4731
not a criterion of logical propositions, 6.1271
of mathematical propositions,
6.2341
Sense
and deducibility, 5.122
cannot be supplied by assertion, 4.064
characterized by expressions,
3.31 (1)
connexion with method of projection, 3.11 (2)
equated with representation of
state of affairs, 4.031 (2)
expressible only by facts, 3.142
new, how communicated,
4.03 (1)
objects occurring in, 4.1211 (1)
of propositional sign, needs no
explanation, 4.02, 4.021
of propositions
and possibilities of existence
of atomic facts, 4.2
contained in sense of other
propositions, 5.122
expressed by spatial position, 3.1431 (2)
form only of, contained in
proposition, 3.13 (4)

Sense—*continued*

how determined, 4.063 (2)

independent of facts, 4.061 (1)

of truth-functions as a function, 5.2341 (1)

only propositions have it, 3.3

opposite, 4.0621 (3)

postulate of determinateness of, 3.23

requires substance, 2.0211

reversed by denial, 5.2341 (3)

what a picture represents is its, 2.221

Senseless (*Sinnlos*)

distinct from nonsensical, 4.461 (3), 4.4611

examples of the, 4.1272 (9), 4.1274, 5.1362 (2)

" laws of inference " are, 5.132 (4)

tautology and contradiction are, 4.461 (3)

Series, formal (*See* Formal series)

Showing

by tautologies and contradictions, 4.461 (1)

by structure, 4.1211 (2)

correctness of solipsism, 5.62 (2)

examples of, 4.1211, 6.12, 6.1201, 6.127 (2), 6.36 (2)

excludes saying, 4.1212

generality, 5.1311 (2)

logic of the world, 6.22

logical form, 4.121 (4)

needed for form of representation, 2.172

of operations, 5.24 (1)

of sense, 4,022

that a formal concept applies, 4.126 (3)

that internal properties hold, 4.122 (4)

that one proposition follows from another, 4.1211 (2)

that the world is my world, 5.62 (3)

the inexpressible, 6.522

what it says, by proposition, 4.461 (1)

Sight, field of, 5.633, 5.6331

Sign

and symbol, 3.326

application of, 3.262

as likeness of the signified, 4.012

as perceptible part of symbol, 3.11, 3.32

cannot receive a wrong sense, 5.4732

complex, 3.1432

equivalence of, 5.47321 (2)

how it determines a logical form, 3.327

identity of tokens of, 3.203

possible, 5.473 (2)

primitive (*See* Primitive signs)

propositional (*See* Propositional sign)

simple, 3.201, 3.202

the same, may belong to different symbols, 3.321

unused, 3.328 (1)

Similes, 4.015

Simplicity of objects, 2.02, 2.021

" Socrates is identical ", 5.473 (2), 5.4733 (3)

Solipsism

coincides with realism, 5.64

correct in intention, 5.62

Soul, 5.5421 (*See also* Subject)

Space

a form of objects, 2.0251

congruence in, 6.36111

geometrical figures cannot contradict laws of, 3.032

logical (*See* Logical space)

spatial objects must lie in, 2.0131 (1)

spatial objects unthinkable apart from, 2.0121 (4)

symmetry in, 6.3611 (3)

visual, 2.0131 (2)

" Spatial spectacles ", 4.0412

INDEX

States of affairs (*Sachlage*)
  can be described, not named,
    3.144 (1)
  connexion of object with,
    2.0122
  possibility of, 2.014
Structure
  and form, 2,033
  and internal property, 4.122(2)
  connexion with operation, 5.22
  logical, 4.014 (2)
  logical relations shown by,
    4.1211 (2)
  of a picture, 2.15 (2)
  of atomic fact, 2,032, 2.034
  of propositions, and deduci-
    bility, 5.13
  of propositions, stand in in-
    ternal relations, 5.2
  properties of, and tautology,
    6.12 (3)
Subject, the
  and the body, 5.631 (2)
  does not belong to the world,
    5.632
  is a limit of the world, 5.632,
    5.641 (3)
  no such thing exists, 5.542 (1),
    5.631 (1)
Substance
  of the world, identified with
    objects, 2.021
  exists independently of what
    is the case, 2.024
  is form and content, 2.025
Successor, definition of, 4.1252(4)
Superstition, 5.1361 (2)
Symbolizing, methods of, 3.322
Symbols
  and signs, 3.326
  as equivalent to rules, 5.541
  composite, criterion of,
    5.5261 (2)
  difference of, 3.323 (3)
  different, may have common
    sign, 3.321
  equated with expressions, 3.31

essential features of, 3.34
for complexes, how defined,
  3.24 (4)
have sign for perceptible part,
  3.32
presuppositions of, 5.5151 (3)
what signifies in, 3.344

Tautology
  a limiting case of combinations
    of symbols, 4.466 (1)
  an ungeneralized proposition
    can be, 6.1231 (2)
  and properties of structure,
    6.12 (3)
  as showing logic of the world,
    6.22
  defined, 4.46 (4)
  derivation of tautology from,
    6.126 (3)
  effect of adjoining, to a pro-
    position, 4.465
  follows from all propositions,
    5.142
  has no truth conditions,
    4.461 (2)
  how used in demonstrating
    logical properties, 6.121
  is analytical proposition, 6.11
  is without sense, 4.461 (3)
  its truth certain, 4.464 (1)
  logical proposition is, 6.1
  method for recognizing, 6.1203
  not a picture of reality, 4.462
  not nonsensical, 4.4611
  probability of, 5.152 (4)
  says nothing, 4.461 (1), 5.142,
    6.11
  shared by propositions,
    5.143 (1)
  shows that it is a tautology,
    6.127 (2)
Theory of knowledge, how related to psychology and
  philosophy, 4.1121 (2)
Theory of types, 3.331-3.333,
  5.252, 6.123 (2)

INDEX

Things (*See* Objects)

Thinkable
and picturable, 3.001
and possible, 3.02
is demarcated by philosophy,
4.114
only uniform connexions are,
6.361

Thought
a priori, criterion of, 3.04
as a logical picture, 3
as method of projection,
3.11 (2)
contains possibility of a state
of affairs, 3.02 (1)
disguised by language, 4.002(4)
expressed by signs, 3.1
form of, 4.002 (4)
how expressed in propositions,
3.2
is applied propositional sign,
3.5
is the significant proposition, 4

Time
a form of objects, 2.0251
" passage " of, 6.3611 (1)
sequence of events in,
6.3611 (1, 2)
temporal objects unthinkable
apart from, 2.0121 (4)

Totality of atomic facts, 2.05

Translation
and projection, 4.0141
as criterion for " what is
common " to symbols,
3.343

Truth
and falsity, not coordinate
relations, 4.061
concept of, explained, 4.063
concept of, Frege's account
false, 4.431 (3)
its connexion with pictorial
nature of proposition, 4.06
not a property, 6.111

Truth-arguments, elementary
propositions are, 5.01

Truth-conditions
groups of, can be ordered in a
series, 4.45
how expressed, 4.442 (4)
of propositions, and truth
possibilities of elementary
propositions, 4.41
symbolism for, 4.43
relation to truth-possibilities,
4.431 (1)

Truth-functions
and truth-operations, 5.3 (2, 3)
are results of operations, 5.234
can be ordered in series, 5.1 (1)
general form of, 6 (1)
not material functions, 5.44 (1)
notations for, 3.3441
of two variables, itemized,
5.101 (1)
result from application of
simultaneous denial,
5.5 (1)
the term introduced, 5.

Truth-grounds
and deducibility, 5.11, 5.12,
5.121
as measure of probability, 5.15,
5.151
defined, 5.101 (2)

Truth-operations
and truth-functions, 5.3 (2, 3)
defined, 5.234

Truth-possibilities
defined, 4.3
of combinations of elementary
propositions, 4.28
schemata for, 4.31

Understanding
depends on understanding
elementary propositions,
4.411
of general propositions depends
on understanding elemen-
tary propositions, 4.411
of names, 4.243
of propositions, 4.02, 4.024

INDEX

of synonyms, 4.243

Unspeakable, the, and philosophy, 4.115

Value, 6.4, 6.41

Variable (*See also* Propositional variable)

an expression presented by, 3.313

is sign of formal concepts, 4.1271

can be regarded as propositional variable, 3.314

determination of values of, 3.317

form of, 4.1271 (2)

general propositional, 5.242

general propositional form is a, 4.53

in expression of general term of series, 5.2522

names, as sign for pseudo-concept, *object*, 4.1272 (1)

name, can be conceived as propositional variable, 3.314 (2)

needed for expressing general term of formal series, 4.1273 (1)

propositional (*See* Propositional variable)

used for operations, 5.24 (1)

values of, 3.315, 5.501 (6)

Whitehead, 5.452 (2), 5.252

Will, the, 6.423, 6.43

Words, cannot occur both in and out of propositions, 2.0122

World, my

I am, 5.63

limits of, 5.62 (3)

World, the

and life are one, 5.621

and logical space, 1.13

and what is the case, 1

completely described by totality of true elementary propositions, 4.26

composed of facts, not things, 1.1

connexion with logical propositions, 6.124

divides into facts, 1.2

independent of my will, 6.373, 6.374

information about, given by simplicity of description, 6.342 (2)

is total reality, 2.063

is totality of atomic facts, 2.04

its form consists of objects, 2.023

limits of, 5.61 (1)

logic of, shown in tautologies and equations, 6.22

logical properties of, 6.12, 6.124

names not needed for description of, 5.526

nature of, revealed by possibility, 3.3421

objects its substance, 2.021

projective relation of propositional sign to, 3.12

sense of, 6.41 (1)

the subject does not belong to it, 5.632

" Zero-method ", in logic, 6.121 (2)